S0-BJJ-841

PORTRAIT OF A SPY

What motivates a man to serve in the shadowy world of espionage? Why does he want to be involved with information of shattering importance to world events? When does he decide to use what he knows—for his own profit and to influence nations' policies?

AN AGENT IN PLACE

offers a psychological portrait of a double agent, a description unequaled in spy fiction, a sense of what it is like to serve the two most powerful nations on earth—at the same time . . .

⊞ ESPIONAGE/INTELLIGENCE LIBRARY ⊞

THE WENNERSTRÖM AFFAIR

AN AGENT IN PLACE

THOMAS WHITESIDE

BALLANTINE BOOKS • NEW YORK

The contents of this book first appeared, in slightly different
    form, in *The New Yorker*.

Library of Congress Catalog Card Number: 66-15907

ISBN 0-345-30326-1

Manufactured in the United States of America

First Ballantine Books Edition: March 1983

To the memory of my friend
JACQUES KATEL

AUTHOR'S NOTE

In pursuing the research for this book, I spent several weeks in Stockholm interviewing security officials and people who had known Colonel Wennerström, or had knowledge of the Wennerström affair. Some of these Swedes in official positions I found stiff and reticent on the subject, but most of them were very friendly and helpful. This cooperation, I should note, extended up to, but not an inch farther than, the line that divides classified from unclassified information. From first to last during my researches into this very delicate subject, in Sweden and in the United States, I was determined neither to seek out nor to accept any off-the-record information (except, in several cases, the names and titles of my informants), nor to make use of any material that I considered might be harmful either to Swedish or American security. I also made it clear to each person I talked to that he would have no access to my manuscript before publication. And I believe I have been able to adhere to this working scheme.

T. W.

April 1966

One

_____

OF ALL THE SPY CASES THAT HAVE BEEN BROUGHT TO
public attention in recent years, few have appeared to
possess such a thoroughly international character as
that of Colonel Stig Erik Constans Wennerström, a
Swedish Air Force officer who was arrested by his
country's security police on June 20, 1963, and charged
with "gross espionage." At first, Wennerström, a man
of coolly elegant demeanor, denied the charges against
him, but after a couple of days he announced that he
had decided to tell the truth. He thereupon started
talking, and went on talking for months—the Swedish
authorities have made public only censored transcripts
of his pre-trial interrogation, yet even these cover more
than three thousand typewritten pages—giving an account of fifteen years of espionage activities that extended far beyond Swedish affairs and, according to
him, embraced some of the broadest strategic mat⸍
in the Cold War.

Colonel Wennerström, who at the time of his arrest was serving as an adviser on disarmament questions at the Swedish Foreign Office, had served as Swedish air attaché both in Moscow and in Washington. He had had a reputation among American diplomats who came in contact with him for being one of the more pro-American Swedish officers, and a man not averse to giving out useful information on Soviet military affairs. Yet from 1948 until 1963, he told his interrogators, he had been a member of the Soviet Intelligence service, in which he secretly held the rank of major general. For a time, in Moscow, he had also acted, he said, in a dual capacity, spying for the Americans against the Soviet Union and simultaneously giving Soviet Intelligence an intimate view of the strategic planning of the Americans and of the North Atlantic Treaty Organization. He said that in the United States he had spied extensively for the Soviets under cover of his official job, bribing people in defense plants throughout this country in order to further his purpose, and turning vast quantities of microfilmed information on our military aviation projects over to a Soviet diplomat in Washington. He told of passing microfilm material to his Soviet contact in the Pentagon itself, and of handing over information that covered the most detailed secret characteristics of American guided missiles. He said that, exploiting his good standing with high American military and diplomatic personnel in Washington, Stockholm, and West Germany, he had been able to supply the Russians with reports on American intentions during a number of international crises, from the recurrent ones in Berlin to the Cuban missile crisis in 1962—reports that he said Soviet Intelligence regarded as important contributions toward the adoption of a realistic Soviet policy on those occasions. And, finally, Wennerström's interrogators, though they were naturally skeptical about taking at face value the accounts of a man who claimed to have spied for both East and West, discovered it to be indubitably true that, in his last period of espionage activity, in his own country, he had given the Soviets so much secret information about Sweden's defenses that the country's entire system of protection against aerial attack had been seriously compromised.

After this long confession came an elaborate investigation, and then Wennerström was tried in secret before a Stockholm magistrate's court in 1964, was found guilty, and was sentenced to life imprisonment. His arrest and conviction were a severe blow to the Swedes, who found it almost inconceivable that a man in Wennerström's highly responsible position—and a man, moreover, who was the son of a regular officer in the coast artillery and was himself a well-trusted member of the exceptionally honor-conscious Swedish officer corps—could have betrayed his own ultra-democratic country and the cause of all the Western democracies, and could have done so undetected for all those years in such a systematic and apparently vastly successful fashion. Why, and just how, such a man could have committed such acts still puzzles a great many people, not only in Sweden but in the entire West.

Wennerström's family background was a bourgeois one. At the time of his birth, in 1906, his father was a captain assigned to the Vaxholm Fortress, outside the entrance to Stockholm Harbor. According to Wennerström's own account, he grew up "in an ordinary officer's home, where there were no excessive or remarkable habits of any sort." Boyhood friends remember him as neat, well-behaved ("correct" was the more usual term), physically unadventurous, and distinctly

ambitious in his schoolwork. When Wennerström was
in his twenties, he decided on a career as a military
flier—a decision that, in spite of the family tradition
of military service, surprised some of his acquaintances when they heard about it. One of them, a woman
now in her late sixties, has recalled feeling that Wennerström was much too "overcautious" for such a career. Wennerström entered the Navy as a cadet in
1929, and a year later he applied for pilot training with
the Air Force. His application was approved, and,
pending his transfer, he was assigned to duty during
the winter of 1930–31 at the naval base at Karlskrona.

As things turned out, these months played an important part in the shaping of his career. He and his
fellow-officers had a fair amount of free time on their
hands, and to fill some of it usefully the Navy offered
them a chance to enroll in various foreign-language
courses. Wennerström signed up for one, and the language he chose to learn was Russian. He already spoke
German quite fluently, because he had spent a number
of his vacations in Germany, and what mainly prompted
him to try his hand at Russian, he later said, was the
fact that an uncle who knew Russian had advised him
that it probably would be useful in his military career.
Wennerström went at his Russian studies diligently
and finished with good marks. Then he went to flying
school, according to plan, and for the next three years
he served as a pilot with the Air Force, although he
was still a naval officer. His instructor in flying school,
Lage Thunberg, who is now Chief of the Swedish Air
Force, has recalled that Wennerström did not seem to
have the makings of a particularly able pilot and, in
addition, was rather pedantic and hard to get to know.

During this period, Wennerström seems to have kept
up his Russian, at least to some extent, and he took
it up again in earnest toward the end of 1933, upon

learning that the Swedish Department of Defense was making available to interested officers a limited number of scholarships for language study abroad. One of these was for the study of Russian in the Baltic states, and when Wennerström applied for it, he was sent to Riga, Latvia, and spent the winter there with a succession of Russian-speaking families. Wennerström's sojourn in Riga had an important bearing on his future for reasons other than the increased knowledge it gave him of Russian. For one thing, because he was formally attached to the military staff at the Swedish Legation, he was eligible to be invited to large diplomatic receptions, and at these and similar social affairs he struck up a number of acquaintanceships, and he found himself highly attracted to what he saw of diplomatic life. For another thing, he came into contact with the Swedish military attachés, who gave him interesting insights into the legitimate intelligence work that they carried on.

Finally, according to what he told his pre-trial interrogators, his stay in Riga enabled him to get a glimpse of covert international intelligence activity. In Riga, he said, he became acquainted with a young American officer who was ostensibly studying Russian, pretty much as Wennerström himself was. But the American, according to Wennerström, revealed himself to be in fact an agent of the British Intelligence service, who for the previous two years had been instructed about Soviet conditions at a secret spot on the French Riviera and who was now assigned to keep track of conditions on the Latvian-Soviet border. In the course of his work, it seemed, this agent occasionally ventured into Soviet territory wearing a Latvian military uniform and, with the connivance of Latvian officers, passing as a member of a Latvian military delegation on an official mission across the border. "It was the first time that I got the least idea that such things as this really existed," Wennerström later recalled. After he had been in Riga awhile, he, too, developed close relations with members of the Latvian military, he said, and they offered him a similar opportunity to make an excursion with them, in Latvian uniform, into Soviet territory. Wennerström did not accept the offer, but according to what he later told his interrogators, it had an "adventurously seductive" effect on his attitude toward intelligence work.

Back in Sweden after his stay in Riga, Wennerström was formally transferred from the Navy to the Air Force, and after a period of higher staff training he was assigned to service on the Air Staff. By 1939, when the Second World War broke out, he was a captain, and in 1940, when the Swedish government decided to assign an air attaché, for the first time, to its embassy in Moscow, Wennerström's general ability as a staff officer, his inclination toward the diplomatic life, and his knowledge of Russian qualified him, in the opinion of his superiors, for the job.

That December, Wennerström, accompanied by his wife, the former Ulla Margareta Carlsson, whom he had married about a year earlier, arrived in Moscow to take up his new post. The prevailing mood in Moscow was extremely tense and grim. The first Russian-Finnish war was over and the Nazi-Soviet non-aggression pact was still in effect. But, with France having fallen and England's cities under dreadful aerial bombardment, most people in Moscow believed, in spite of the insistent Russian propaganda line that the conflict in the West merely represented an intramural capitalistic quarrel and was no business of the Soviet Union, that war with Germany was ominously close. In this on-the-eve atmosphere, the Moscow diplomatic corps was in a turbulent state, for it consisted of all

sorts of fiercely contending elements: the representatives of the European warring powers, Germany, Italy,
France, and Britain; those of China and Japan, then
fighting each other in Asia; and those of the currently
non-belligerent powers, including the United States
and the Soviet Union itself. Perhaps half the diplomatic
corps consisted of people who were politically ranged
against one another as deadly enemies, and every com-
ponent of the corps was feverishly at work negotiating,
scheming, and observing in furtherance of its own
national policies and those of its actual or potential
allies. The situation probably appeared at its most tan-
gled when the Russians, adhering to the diplomatic
practices of a country at peace, simultaneously invited
members of both the Allied and the Axis blocs, along
with the neutrals, to large diplomatic receptions. At
these affairs, many of the groups of guests did not
recognize each other's presence and stayed off in cor-
ners of their own, only the neutrals being able to move
freely from group to group. Because of this mobility
and the amount of information they were able to pick
up in their official and social rounds, the neutrals were
much sought after as intelligence sources.

The new Swedish air attaché was no exception.
"One might say that everybody asked us all about
everything," Wennerström told his interrogators.
Among the neutrals, it appears, there was a good deal
of competition over who could latch on to available
scraps of information first and thereby acquire the reputation of being a good source; some of the attachés
would discreetly trade a piece of information they had
picked up from one diplomat for a scrap from another
diplomat. Wennerström, as he came to know more
people, grew particularly active in this field, and he
found that, with his fluent command of German, he
was especially successful in dealing with the German

military mission. For their part, the Germans in Moscow certainly had good reason to maintain friendly contact with any neutral who would talk to them; the movements of the German diplomats within Russia were paralyzed by Russian restrictions, and the German Embassy was under the strictest Russian security surveillance. Consequently, the Germans were only too ready to help Wennerström out by giving him military information about the Soviet Union in exchange for anything he was able to give them.

Wennerström's own official concerns centered on the obtaining of information about the size and the organization of the Soviet Air Force. In particular, his supervisors had instructed him to collect whatever maps and reference books he could that had to do with the border region between the Soviet Union and Finland, where the Russians were known to have built a number of new military airfields. In order to obtain some of this material, which was extremely scarce, Wennerström undertook a scouting trip on the Leningrad-Murmansk railroad, having gained permission for the journey from the Soviet authorities by telling them that he needed to visit a Swedish ship docked at Murmansk. On the journey, he obtained some map data useful to the Swedes, but before sending this off to Stockholm by diplomatic pouch he surreptitiously passed it to the Germans, who, he recalled more than twenty years later, found it of great intelligence value and photographed it for transmission to Berlin before returning it.

Then, during another trip Wennerström made outside Moscow on official Swedish business, this time to Kiev, he picked up information identifying a high Russian military staff group that had moved into a hotel there, and as soon as he returned to Moscow he passed this information along to the Germans, who were eagerly seeking details on troop concentrations in the Ukraine. According to Wennerström, this intelligence was immediately relayed to Berlin, and, in view of the slaughter that took place in the Ukraine after the German invasion of Russia, Wennerström was sure that the information he handed over was of the first importance. In return for such intelligence data, he says, he obtained from the Germans information on the Soviet Navy in the Baltic, which he passed on to Stockholm; also, in recognition of his services in allowing them to photograph the Soviet maps he collected on his Murmansk trip, the Germans gave him an opportunity to buy rubles from them at an exceptionally low rate.

Wennerström's superiors in Moscow seem to have been quite unaware of the extent of his involvement with the Germans. Colonel Engelbrekt Flodström, the Swedish military attaché in Moscow in those days, has recalled that Wennerström was altogether secretive with his colleagues about the persons he met on his rounds of diplomatic duty; Flodström assumed at the time, he has said, that Wennerström, in careerist fashion, was trying to keep whatever information he gathered close to his chest so as to claim the maximum personal credit when he reported to his superiors in Stockholm. Wennerström has denied that in this period he considered himself an agent of a foreign power, saying, "I carried on my contacts within my profession to the extent that seemed suitable, even though it is easy to see that [between permissible and impermissible activities] there was no sharp borderline."

Wennerström stayed in Moscow until March 1941, when the Swedish military mission there was temporarily reduced to one officer. Returning to Stockholm, he was assigned to the Defense Staff as an Air Intelligence officer. His superiors expected to reassign him to Moscow after a time, but when war broke out between Germany and the Soviet Union, this plan was abandoned. However, Wennerström continued to be formally accredited to the Soviet government, and because of this accreditation his name was put on the diplomatic invitation list of the Soviet Embassy in Stockholm, with the result that he was soon attending social affairs at that embassy and various others. The more prominent of his diplomatic contacts included members of the German military mission in Stockholm, who, having evidently been apprised by Berlin of Wennerström's usefulness in Moscow, eagerly cultivated his acquaintance, so that what he called "a lively association" arose between them. In the course of this association, he passed on to the Germans various items of information that were of importance to them—for example, a report on a Soviet airfield in the Murmansk region—that had their primary origin in current reports by the Swedish military attaché in Moscow. These pieces of intelligence, Wennerström was told, were immediately cabled to Berlin.

While this association with the Germans continued, Wennerström was also developing his connections with members of the Russian Legation in Stockholm, and, in particular, with the Soviet Minister there, Mme. Alexandra Kollantai. After the Soviet Union entered the war, a number of Soviet sailors and airmen who had been shipwrecked or shot down in Sweden were interned in various camps there. From time to time, Mme. Kollantai made a tour of the camps, and on some of these occasions Wennerström, because of his knowledge of Russian and his acquaintance with the Minister, was chosen as the escorting officer. After a while, he says, he got to know her "extremely well."

He also became well acquainted with Colonel Nikolai Nikitushev, the Soviet air attaché.

Wennerström's contacts with the Germans and the Russians ceased temporarily in the fall of 1943, when he was transferred to Såtenäs, in the south of Sweden, for flight duty, but this assignment brought him into close contact with military people of yet another nationality—Americans. Såtenäs was then an assembly point for American bombers that had made forced landings in Swedish territory after bombing runs over Germany, and as Wennerström carried out his duties at Såtenäs he came to know a number of American Air Force officers.

After two years, Wennerström was reassigned to Stockholm, with the rank of major, but since this was the fall of 1945, his old friends from the German Embassy were no longer there. He quickly reestablished himself in Stockholm diplomatic life, however, and this time, through his friendship with American officers he had met at Såtenäs, he became a frequent guest at United States Embassy receptions. At the same time, he was receiving invitations to social affairs at the Soviet Embassy, just as before, and he often acted as an escorting officer for Russian defense attachés at air shows and the like in Sweden. In 1946, after the Swedes had shown the Russian air attaché and others some of the first Swedish jet planes, the Russians reciprocated by agreeing to invite a Swedish officer to attend a Soviet air show outside Moscow at which the Russians would display some of *their* first jets. Wennerström received the assignment.

Wennerström told his interrogators after his arrest in 1963 that shortly before he left for the Soviet Union he was approached in Stockholm by a man dressed in civilian clothes, whom he took to be a member of American Intelligence, and who told him that his name had been turned up by the Americans in captured files of the so-called Gehlen organization (a German intelligence agency that had dealt with Soviet and Eastern European affairs during the Second World War, and that in postwar years was partly reconstituted under United States control as a West German intelligence agency) in which he was listed as a "valuable contact." The man added that the matter was known to all the principal American officials in Stockholm with whom Wennerström had come into contact. "Naturally, it was decidedly uncomfortable to learn in this way that one's name had been rambling around and had wandered into Germany, and then drifted across the Atlantic, and then strayed back into Europe and . . . to Stockholm," Wennerström has said. According to Wennerström, the agent, having confronted him with this information, went on to say that since in the past Wennerström had, in effect, worked against the Soviet Union by working in favor of Germany, and since he had in recent times developed such friendly relations with the Americans, it would now seem reasonable for him to agree to be of help to the United States. Next, the agent, by Wennerström's account obviously aware of his coming trip to the Soviet Union, remarked on the opportunity he would have, as a neutral, to move about there with comparative freedom, and proposed that he agree to mail a certain parcel in Leningrad on his way to Moscow. Wennerström told his interrogators that he accepted the assignment and mailed the parcel—which he understood to contain radio tubes, or some sort of equipment that might be used in a clandestine radio transmitter—without difficulty. On his return to Stockholm, he said, he had no further contact with the presumed American agent, and his close relations with both the American and the Soviet Embassies continued pretty much as before.

At the beginning of 1948, the head of the Swedish Air Force, General Bengt Nordenskiöld, told Wennerström, who had recently been promoted to lieutenant colonel, that he thought the time had come to assign an air attaché to the Swedish Embassy in Moscow once more, and that Wennerström still seemed the logical man for the job, especially since he had established such good relations with Colonel Ivan Petrovich Rybachenko, who in 1943 had succeeded Nikitushev as Soviet air attaché in Stockholm. And the general had additional reasons for proposing the assignment, he told Wennerström. The fact seems to have been that Wennerström's future as a flying officer did not look very good. General Nordenskiöld wanted all his senior officers to be enthusiastic and skillful pilots, and Wennerström had been involved in a couple of flying accidents. His next promotion would logically have been to the position of wing commander, but now, the general let him know, the outlook for his getting it was very uncertain, and the Moscow post seemed the best alternative. Wennerström, very much disappointed to hear that his promotion was unlikely, accepted the proposed assignment. In the following weeks, he busied himself with preliminary technical studies at the headquarters of the Swedish Air Force, and in doing so, he has said, he became involved in long talks with an Intelligence officer about espionage. They discussed various kinds, including what Wennerström was to characterize as "the most advanced and most dangerous form of agent work"—that done by the kind of *provocateur* who is planted by one power in the espionage service of another. This kind of activity is especially dangerous for the power that initiates it, inasmuch as the agent may be secretly enlisted by the other power, and "doubled" back upon his original employer—hence the term "double agent." The talks also involved a detailed discussion of the Russian methods of recruiting agents and of Western counter-espionage techniques. Wennerström appears to have been highly impressed by his colleague's revelations of the extent and complexity of postwar espionage. As a result of this, he later said, "there was awakened in me the idea of trying something of this sort myself. . . . I realized that I stood very well with the Russians." Specifically, he has said, he started to wonder whether he might not have an opportunity to penetrate the Soviet Intelligence service on behalf of Sweden.

Whatever it was that had been awakened in Wennerström's mind soon assumed the shape of action—action in regard to his relations with the Russians. With the North Atlantic Treaty Organization in process of formation, the Russians were concerning themselves energetically with the system of Allied bases that was being built along the perimeter of the Soviet Union, and even though Sweden was not to become a member of NATO, the fact that Sweden was also building new military airfields and expanding existing ones was of great interest to the Soviets. In October of 1948, according to Wennerström's recollection, he became aware that Colonel Rybachenko, the Soviet air attaché, was expressing particular interest in the location of a certain secret Swedish military airfield then under construction. Wennerström said that, having become aware of Rybachenko's interest during a conversation with the Russian, he gradually brought the talk around to such installations, and Rybachenko asked him for details. "I had determined to give him an answer which would appear to be a jesting shrugging off of the question, but which might also be regarded as an invitation," Wennerström has recalled. "I answered, 'Well, if this information about that airfield is so important, I will tell you what I know for five thousand kronor.'"

(The sum is the equivalent of about a thousand dollars.) According to Wennerström, Rybachenko looked at him and, after a pause, said something like "Well, I'll find out about it."

Soon after the conversation, Rybachenko left Stockholm for Moscow. He was absent for some weeks. By the time he returned, Wennerström, by his own account, had "almost forgotten" about their talk, but when next he saw Rybachenko, at a cocktail party, the Russian came up to him and remarked, "The thing is O.K." A few days later, Wennerström encountered Rybachenko at a luncheon, and afterward the Russian offered to drive him home. Wennerström accepted, and when he got out of the car in front of his apartment house, Rybachenko thrust out a hand, gave him a small package, and sped off without a word. The package contained five thousand kronor in bills. During his interrogation, Wennerström described his reaction in this way: "I recall that when I came up into my apartment and then checked the contents of the packet, highly conflicting feelings arose within me. In a fashion, it was satisfying that I had succeeded in my purpose and got at least a foot, so to speak, into the [Soviet Intelligence] organization. But on the other hand it was entirely clear that I was setting out on the most dangerous thing that one could possibly imagine within [the field of] intelligence service." He went on to say that he nevertheless decided, after some thought, to continue following the course he had embarked on. As a consequence, he delivered to Rybachenko a map on which he had put a dot to indicate the site of the airfield in question. After this, Rybachenko asked him if, when he got to Moscow, Wennerström would like to see one of his Russian "old acquaintances." Wennerström said he would, and arrangements for the meeting, which was clearly to be a surreptitious one, were thereupon made.

Wennerström arrived in Moscow in January 1949, and since the routine of his official work was familiar to him, he settled in quickly. One of the assignments the Swedes had given him before he left Stockholm was to find out what he could about heat-resistant alloys that the Russians might be using in their jet engines, and he appears to have gained the impression that this information, if he got it, would ultimately be relayed to the United States Intelligence. Whatever the facts may have been, Wennerström approached the assignment in a secretive fashion. He has said that after searching through the technical literature and visiting various bookstores and libraries he found that the only place he could get the needed data without arousing suspicion was at a specialized library in Leningrad. He arranged a trip to that city, ostensibly for sightseeing purposes, and took along a miniature camera he had bought in Moscow. The library was on a street off the Nevsky Prospekt, and Wennerström said that he was able to enter it without his foreign appearance arousing any particular interest—probably, he explained to his interrogators, because Scandinavian-looking people from an area called Ingermanland, to the west of Leningrad, are a common sight in the city. He has said that in the library he eventually found what he wanted—a technical pamphlet with a number on it indicating that its distribution was restricted—and that, taking this pamphlet to a small unoccupied room he had also found, he photographed the document's pages; then, he said, he returned the pamphlet, without incurring the suspicion of any of the librarians, and went back to Moscow, where he sent off his films to Stockholm by diplomatic courier. Wennerström gave his Swedish colleagues in Moscow some general information about the metallurgical data he had obtained, but while he indicated to them that he had pulled off a coup, he said nothing about how he had obtained the information.

According to the arrangements that Wennerström had made with Rybachenko, he was supposed to meet his "old acquaintance" on a certain Sunday near a statue of Pushkin on Gorky Street. The meeting was set for 2 p.m. For some reason, Wennerström was unable to keep the rendezvous. However, Rybachenko's arrangement with him provided for just this contingency, stipulating that there should be another attempt to meet exactly a week later if either party should fail to make the first date. Wennerström kept the second rendezvous, and there by the statue he found waiting for him—in civilian clothes, as he was—Colonel Nikitushev, the former Soviet air attaché in Stockholm. They shook hands and chatted, in the normal fashion of two old acquaintances out on a stroll. Then, in Wennerström's words, they "walked about in the pleasant neighborhood with flower pots and wide streets," and at one point stopped to reminisce about life in Stockholm. They paused. "Suddenly," according to Wennerström, "a big black car appeared. It was about 2:30 p.m. Nikitushev said, 'Now it is time for a cup of tea. Come, let us go.' The car left at high speed for the outskirts of the city. It was driven this way and that until I was completely confused. Finally, we stopped at a house quite some distance from Moscow....A fine tea table was set in the house. We drank tea alone—alone except for a waiter—and got the usual Russian caviar and vodka besides. After some time, we were rather easy and relaxed."

Next, Wennerström said, they retired to another room to talk. There Nikitushev explained that he had attained a relatively important post in the Soviet Intelligence service, and knew that Wennerström had delivered valuable information to the service through Rybachenko in Stockholm. After that, he got down to business. He began with an exposition of the formation of the North Atlantic Treaty Organization, and the strategic problems that it posed for the Soviet Union. What was particularly uncomfortable from the Soviet point of view, he said, was that "hostile-minded" states were to be seen everywhere, most of them backed by the great power of the United States and its allies. One of the basic problems that the Soviets were confronted with as a consequence of this situation, he explained, was that of determining which of these unfriendly fronts presented serious military dangers. While the Russians, he said, were inclined to believe that for present purposes they did not have to reckon with any threat from the Baltic Sea area—or, at any rate, from the direction of Sweden—they were aware that military discussions had taken place between high military representatives of Denmark, Norway, and Sweden, and Soviet military people were wondering whether a secret agreement might not exist that, in the event of war, would bring Sweden into the hostilities on the side of NATO. Wennerström assured Nikitushev that no such secret agreement existed, and that Sweden fully intended to adhere to its neutral policy. Nikitushev then shifted back to the relationship that had been established between Wennerström and Rybachenko in Stockholm, and said that his chief in the Soviet Intelligence service had asked to meet Wennerström. "It was, of course, not too late to say 'No, thanks' to such a meeting," Wennerström later reported. But he felt that he had burned his bridges, he said, and the notion "that I was going to continue my march behind the curtain of the Soviet Intelligence service" won out.

So he consented to meet Nikitushev's chief, and another rendezvous was agreed upon.

At the appointed hour, Nikitushev was waiting at a new meeting place with the same car and chauffeur. The chauffeur shared the front seat with another man, and when the car drove off, it was followed by a second car. Nikitushev and Wennerström were driven to an apartment on a side street in the center of Moscow, and there Wennerström was asked to remove his hat and overcoat, which, being of foreign cut, would have been noticeable among Muscovites, and he was given Russian replacements. Then the two men again got back into the car, the side and back windows of which were now covered by drawn shades, and were driven to a large apartment building, where two other men were waiting for them. One of them was introduced as Nikitushev's chief. Wennerström testified that he was a general, and that "he served in the headquarters in Moscow that was the directing and coordinating organ for the various sectors within the Intelligence service." The chief's companion, Wennerström has said, was the head of the security service that was responsible for the surveillance of foreign diplomats in Moscow.

Vodka was served, accompanied by caviar and other appetizers, and over the refreshments the officer who had been identified as Nikitushev's chief told Wennerström he was well aware of the fact that many members of the foreign diplomatic corps in Moscow felt isolated from the Russians, and of their complaints that they found it all but impossible to make arrangements to attend such events as lectures on subjects of professional interest to them. He promised to make such contacts easier for Wennerström. Then he took Wennerström into an adjoining room for a private talk. He began by referring to Nikitushev's conversation

with Wennerström about Sweden and NATO, and he,
too, stressed the advantage that accrued to the Soviet
Union from the fact that, with Sweden's continued
neutrality, no front in the Baltic Sea area had to be
reckoned with. He thanked Wennerström for his collaboration with Rybachenko in Stockholm, and pulled
from his pocket the map for which Rybachenko had
paid Wennerström five thousand kronor. On it Wennerström could see the little dot that indicated the position of the Swedish airfield. Then Nikitushev's chief,
Wennerström said, "with a roguish glint in his eyes,
tore the map up and threw the pieces into the waste-
paper basket," explaining that although intelligence
from all quarters of the globe was ordinarily of interest
to the Soviets, under the existing circumstances Wennerström should understand that Sweden could not be
of major interest, so Wennerström need not worry
about having to give information on Swedish affairs;
the Soviet Union was interested in entirely different
matters. It was the United States, the chief said, against
which every resource of the Soviet Union had to be
deployed. To this end, the Soviet Union needed to
know all about the principles of the war planning being
undertaken by the United States. Right in Moscow,
the chief continued, members of Western missions
were carrying on intelligence work against the Soviet
Union under the direction of the American Embassy,
and it was of crucial importance to obtain the fullest
possible information about the exact purposes of this
activity. At last, he asked Wennerström whether he
wished to enter the Soviet Intelligence service, with
the mission of finding out what he could about NATO's
war planning against the Soviet Union. He said that
he didn't expect Wennerström to answer offhand—
that he could give an answer any time he wished, and,
indeed, if he didn't want to answer at all, he would

never be bothered again. Now, the general said, it was high time for lunch. During lunch, Wennerström has said, he decided to accept the offer, and he made his decision known to Nikitushev's chief at the end of the meal, when tea and coffee were being served.

Then all four men retired to the adjoining room for a business talk. The chief announced to the two other men that Wennerström was joining the Soviet Intelligence service and would be assigned to its American sector. Losing no time, he designated Nikitushev then and there as Wennerström's regular contact man. Next, he turned to the other man and told him that Wennerström was to be protected against harm from either Western or Soviet security people, and was not to be shadowed by any Soviet security organization other than the one he was working for. Then, addressing Wennerström and Nikitushev, the chief stressed the need for Wennerström to concentrate on the principal task of obtaining information on NATO's war planning from the embassies of the NATO countries and to avoid "scattered effort." He once more assured Wennerström that the affairs of the Swedish Embassy were of no interest to the Soviet Union, and that, in any case, Soviet Intelligence possessed means of obtaining Swedish information on what he called "a higher level." The chief added that while Wennerström was busy working on behalf of Soviet Intelligence, he would naturally be short of time for his legitimate Swedish duties, and he again promised to see to it that Wennerström was given easier access to Soviet sources of information to obviate this difficulty. Finally, saying that he would leave it to Nikitushev and Wennerström to work out the details, the chief took his leave. Wennerström never saw him again.

Wennerström and Nikitushev soon left, too, and were returned by car to the apartment they had pre-

viously stopped at. There Nikitushev gave Wennerström ten thousand rubles as an advance payment for
his work, pointed out on a map nine different spots in
Moscow where he and Wennerström could meet, instructed Wennerström in the procedure for arranging
their meetings, and gave him back his own hat and
overcoat. Formally as well as practically, Wennerström was now a Soviet agent.

To carry out the assignments given him by the Soviets, Wennerström needed to establish a great many
contacts with the various Western embassies in Moscow, and, he told his interrogators, the Russians expected this process to take a long time. However, he
got off to a quick start. One of the military attachés
in the American Embassy had been an acquaintance
of his in Stockholm, and through this man he quickly
"got in," as he put it, at the United States Embassy.
And because of the importance of the Americans within
the diplomatic corps in Moscow, he has said, his entrée
into other diplomatic missions "came almost by itself."
As Wennerström built up his acquaintance within the
diplomatic corps, he reported regularly to his Soviet
contact man on what he observed. According to the
prearranged system, their meetings sometimes took
place on small back streets and sometimes in inner
courts. Nikitushev would be waiting, the car and
chauffeur would be nearby, and the two men would
get into the car and be driven off. If Wennerström had
only a short report to make, the pair would be driven
out to the suburbs of Moscow and back; if he had quite
a long report to make, they would be taken either to
the apartment where he had been paid or to the house
that he had visited the first time he met Nikitushev.
At first, Wennerström recalled, he had the impression
that he had been immediately accepted by the Soviet

Intelligence service, but soon he realized that he was very much on trial. His Soviet contacts seemed to feel that things were going almost too fast, he thought, and they kept cross-checking details of his reports. "For example, I might say that I had been to dinner with a certain person, and that I . . . considered I had established a good contact either with the person or with someone that I met there," Wennerström has said. "Then they checked this by asking, as though in passing, about this person's clothing, or how I or some other person had got there, or who the other guests were, and they might ask about some point in time. Subsequently they could check these data through information they got from other sources."

Wennerström has said he came to feel that it would take him a long time to get through his test period, and, as a result, "I had various thoughts about whether it would be a good thing if I could pull off more or less a sort of coup, which would at once make me accepted." An opportunity for such a coup soon arose. In the spring of 1949, Wennerström was due to return to Stockholm for a few weeks, on official Swedish business, and before he left Moscow he had a meeting with Nikitushev, who told him that an important Soviet conference on strategy was to take place shortly, and that the Intelligence service woud be required to present position papers on the Baltic Sea front. He asked Wennerström to seek information that might verify or correct the estimate that this front presented no military threat to the Soviet Union. He said that if Wennerström did obtain such information, he should give it to Rybachenko, who was still the Soviet air attaché in Stockholm, and that if in Wennerström's estimation the information should have high priority for transmission to Moscow he should give Rybachenko the password "Lightning."

Among the people Wennerström talked with on his return to Stockholm was an officer who, to judge from Wennerström's account of the conversation, may have been the same Swedish officer with whom he had originally discussed the structure of the Soviet Intelligence service. Wennerström told his interrogators that when he approached this man once more, he "continued to have normal feelings of loyalty" to Sweden, and that he thought of resuming their earlier conversation about the structure and recruiting methods of Soviet Intelligence and the role of foreign agents who might penetrate that service. "I had thought I would say that I had absorbed what he had spoken of . . . and that I myself had had a try at [being recruited by the Russians] in Moscow, and that it had been successful," Wennerström testified. However, after the conversation had been under way for a while "there came into play psychological . . . factors which upset my original ideas."

The censored report of Wennerström's pre-trial interrogation indicates that he believed his fellow-officer to be acting, officially or unofficially, as a contact with American Military Intelligence. And it seemed that after the two had been talking for a time the other man asked Wennerström where he had obtained the data on Russian jet-airplane alloys, and that Wennerström stubbornly declined to give any information about his source, on the ground that if he did so, "others"— presumably including the Americans—would probably make a beeline for that source and thus compromise it. "When [the other officer] realized that he would not be able to tell his contact man in the United States about the source of my information, he became extraordinarily annoyed," Wennerström said in recalling the scene. "One may say that his attitude was that of a dissatisfied superior toward an erring subordinate.... I was the sub-agent and he was the agent." Wennerström said that as this impression sank into his mind, "this relationship caused me to rage inwardly in a pronounced fashion." And in his interrogation he recalled some of the factors that contributed to this seething reaction: "At the moment, I was in a touchy state.... I had been passed over in the appointments to wing chief. Unfortunately, [in such a] situation one soon feels distinctly that one has been slighted. One feels that one is out of the game and made an exception of. One no longer has any influence, and hardly anyone pays attention to the views one expresses, et cetera." As for his impression that he was being made to play the part of a sub-agent for the Americans, he said it occurred to him right away that he had no need for a line of contact with the Americans that went via the other officer—and, in fact, that "there was no reason why I should not get myself a direct [American] contact and be my own master." He explained, "I was tired of playing a subordinate part and I wanted to make an end to this as quickly as possible. Therefore I made a right-about-turn in the course of my thoughts.... I said nothing about my contacts with the Soviet Intelligence service."

Strong as his feelings were, Wennerström remained outwardly calm, and soon, he testified, the talk veered from his refusal to reveal his source of information to the subject of the technical material that his Swedish superiors wanted him to obtain when he returned to the Soviet Union, and from there it turned to the subject of Swedish strategy and the sort of information that the Swedish military required from attachés abroad. At this point, the other officer told Wennerström about a top-secret outline of the Swedish Defense Staff's strategic plans in the event of war. Wennerström has said that "a spark lighted up within" him when he heard of this. "Why," he later explained, "here was a splendid opportunity to carry off something that would be of special value for the Soviet Intelligence service to study before [the Soviet conference on strategy]. And here, unquestionably, was something calculated to increase my prestige all of a sudden." In consequence, he said, he worked the conversation around in such a way that the Swedish officer agreed when he suggested that the strategic analysis be placed on the list of military documents he was to study during his weeks in Stockholm.

A few days later, Wennerström obtained a copy of this document, and one evening not long afterward he passed it to Rybachenko for photographing, and gave him the password "Lightning." The original was returned to Wennerström the next day. It must have consisted of a huge bundle of material, for Wennerström testified that upon his return to Moscow he learned that a whole planeload of Swedish-language translators had been flown from Leningrad to Moscow when it was received. How the Russians evaluated its importance Wennerström was able to judge very quickly. No sooner had he returned to Moscow and made contact with Nikitushev again than he realized that he had achieved his goal of "getting out of the backwater that the test period in the Soviet Intelligence service constituted." Nikitushev told him, he has said, that his transmission of the Swedish document was regarded in the highest ranks of Soviet Intelligence as a great coup. As an indication of the importance of that information, Nikitushev said, Wennerström had been given a code name—a distinction that was accorded only the more prominent Soviet agents. The code name was Eagle.

Two

_____

WITHIN A SHORT TIME, WENNERSTRÖM RECEIVED further signs of Soviet appreciation. He was told that henceforth his dealings with the Soviet Intelligence service would be on a higher level, and that, although he and Nikitushev might still communicate on certain matters, the latter was to be replaced as his Soviet contact man by an officer who was identified to him as a general from the American sector of Soviet Intelligence. Wennerström was also made the beneficiary of what he has described as "certain more expensive steps" in security. For example a special telephone line was established to facilitate his reaching his new contact man. "It was very ingeniously arranged," Wennerström has said. "I was the only person who knew the number. There was someone on the other end twenty-four hours a day. So they knew that only I could ring them. In order to protect themselves against a wrong number, they had decided that I should first ring and let three buzzes pass by and hang up the receiver, then ring again and pass my message. I needed never say who I was. Furthermore, I was to call only from telephone booths in the city, the purpose being to prevent tapping." Also, he was told, two cars would now be constantly available to his new contact man. In case Wennerström had to be reached in a hurry, one of the cars would park outside his house or outside his office, and whenever Wennerström saw the car in one of these places (he had memorized the license numbers, and he knew the drivers by sight), he was to telephone his contact man immediately. If Wennerström was on the move when a contact had to be made, one of the cars would overtake him and stop at the curb, and this, too, meant that Wennerström was to phone—unless his contact man was sitting in the car, in which case Wennerström would join him for a conference.

Wennerström's new contact man appears to have been a remarkable person in many ways. There is no doubt that he exerted a strong influence on Wennerström, who came to regard him as one of his closest friends. The name by which Wennerström knew him, and heard him addressed in the company of others, was Lemenov, and he used the given name and patronymic of Pyotr Pavlovich, but, Wennerström testified, he never knew whether or not this was the man's real name, and in the record of Wennerström's pre-trial interrogation in Stockholm his contact is usually referred to merely as "the General." Wennerström said of him, "He was undoubtedly a considerable personality. He was calm and serious and talked in a strikingly deep voice. He had an altogether unique ability of arousing those around him to enthusiasm, and of sweeping those around him along with him. . . . I [occasionally] saw him amid a fairly large company, and the same thing was true there. At times one had the impression that he had an almost hypnotic ability to carry people along."

Under the General's orders, Wennerström set about cultivating his acquaintances at the American Embassy so as to obtain information there that he could pass on. His respect for the General notwithstanding, it appears from his own testimony that he did not tell his Soviet contact man as much about his relations with the Americans as he might have. According to what he told his Swedish interrogators after his arrest, he began—at the very time he was pushing ahead with his work on behalf of Soviet Intelligence—to do what he could to fulfill the urge that had seized him in Stockholm, to "get myself a direct contact" with American Military Intelligence and "become my own master." Shortly after he returned to Moscow, he said, he was approached by an American air attaché, who said he had learned from Washington that Wennerström had managed to acquire valuable information in the Soviet Union from an unknown source, and that Washington was eager to know what that source was. Wennerström testified that while he still declined to reveal the source, he did establish further contacts with United States Air Force Intelligence. As a result, he has said, he obtained an agreement whereby he would supply the United States with additional military information about the Soviet Union through an American contact man in Moscow, in return for a certain sum of money, which he asked the Americans to pay him in Italian lire. According to Wennerström, "So far as I personally was concerned this meant that I had achieved my aim; namely, that of being an independent agent."

By his account, the tasks that he carried out on behalf of the Americans were supposed to fit into the framework of a vastly expanded intelligence network

that the United States was building up around the Soviet Union. He has said that this network employed,
among other things, United States aircraft equipped
with special radio transmitters, which patrolled as close
as possible to the borders of the Soviet Union in order
to communicate with resident agents, some of whom
had been parachuted into the country; illegal high-
altitude reconnaissance flights by the RB-36, a prede-
cessor of the U-2; camera-equipped balloons that were
released in Western Europe to drift eastward with the
prevailing winds, automatically taking high-altitude
photographs until they came down in the Pacific, where
many of them were picked up; and, finally, and most
important, the collection of a great mass of information
from miscellaneous sources inside and outside the Soviet Union. Wennerström says that his own efforts on
behalf of American Intelligence were devoted to seeking out information about suitable bombing targets
within the U.S.S.R., and that he was assigned this
task because, as a neutral, he would presumably find
it relatively easy to move about the country.

Moving about the Soviet Union was indeed relatively easy for Wennerström, for when he wanted to
go somewhere, he had only to apply to Nikitushev,
his former contact man, who was under orders to help
him as much as possible in connection with his official
Swedish work, so that he could get on all the faster
with his spying for the Soviets. Ostensibly on Swedish
business, Wennerström made trips to various parts of
the Soviet Union, including Siberia, the Caucasus, and
the Ukraine, and in these places, he claimed, he obtained military information for the Americans. Thus,
he has said, on a trip to Novosibirsk, in Siberia, the
plane in which he was traveling did not land, as he
had expected, at a commercial airfield in the town of
Kazan, but instead made an unscheduled stop at a

military air base east of there. The Americans, he continued, had been highly interested in this particular military field, because they suspected that it was a base for strategic bombers intended for use against American installations along the perimeter of the Soviet Union. When he landed, he said, he observed that the airplanes on the field were the latest type of Soviet strategic bomber. "I took photographs with a telescopic lens from a toilet window at the airport building," he testified. "I turned the film over later to my American contact man. Thanks to the telescopic lens, it was possible to discern all the details of the planes within its range." At the same time, he went on, he was able to pick up another piece of military information that the Americans did not possess. Inside the airport building, he glimpsed on a bulletin board a notice that jobs were available for meteorologists·at an air base at Varlamovo Bay, near Murmansk, on the Arctic Ocean. The notice was marked as having emanated from the staff headquarters of the Soviet Strategic Air Command in Moscow, and Wennerström has said that by putting these facts together he gave the Americans their first intimation of the existence of a Soviet strategic air base at Varlamovo Bay—a point from which Russian bombers could take off on flights over the North Pole to Canada and the United States.

Just as Wennerström did not inform the Soviet Intelligence service of whatever tasks he may have been carrying out for the Americans, he did not tell the Americans about the spying he was doing on behalf of the Soviets. And, of course, he told his Swedish superiors about neither of his extracurricular activities; in fact, it seems that he hardly let his Swedish colleagues in Moscow know what he was doing on behalf of Sweden. He later indicated that in no time he found that his surreptitious activities on behalf of Soviet Intelligence could be made to dovetail nicely with his activities on behalf of United States Intelligence. As an agent of the Soviets, he has said, his initial task, once he had passed through his probationary period, was to obtain information on American military planning against Russia.

His new Soviet contact, the General, began briefing him on this assignment by saying that he was highly pleased with Wennerström for establishing such good contacts within the embassies of the NATO powers in such short order. The General then mentioned that the Russians had been able to discover a great deal about the intelligence work that was being carried on in the Moscow embassies of the NATO powers under the guidance of the Americans, and he went on to say that the important thing was to obtain an evaluation of the aim of such intelligence work, because, together with other similar activities, it could probably provide an indication of NATO's basic war planning against the Soviet Union, and, in particular, could clarify the question of whether the United States planned to use only its air power and nuclear bombs against specific targets or was planning on a land invasion as well. He told Wennerström that, in view of the contacts he had made among the Americans, he seemed to be the person within the Western camp in Moscow most competent to obtain such information. The General needed a brief prepared in time for another Soviet conference on strategy, he said, and he urged Wennerström to concentrate on this task to the exclusion of everything else.

"The task was easier for me than [the General] could ever have thought," Wennerström recalled after his arrest. "Thanks to my role as an agent for both sides . . . it was almost comical. I would get a query from my Soviet contact man that, from his point of view, was fairly hard to answer. When, later on, I would meet my American contact man, I would get a direct reply to the question...as well as a task from him." Thus, Wennerström has remarked, while he was busy gathering information for the Americans on potential bombing targets within the Soviet Union, he was also able at the same time to carry out instructions from Soviet Intelligence to find out what those targets were. He has said that as he came to the Americans with what he called "bits of the jigsaw puzzle" concerning targets, he learned that this information was collated with other data and plotted on a situation map in the American Embassy—a map that he was not allowed to see. However, he told his interrogators, as he turned over to the Soviet Intelligence service whatever he could about the Americans' interest in particular targets, the General set up a target map of his own, on which all the information that Wennerström brought in was marked, along with information from other sources.

According to Wennerström, some of the information relating to presumed targets was for a while quite puzzling to the Soviets. By way of illustration, he described a trip he made to Odessa with the ostensible purpose of visiting a scientific institute there but with the actual purpose of carrying out an American Intelligence assignment. "The task given me by the Americans seemed almost laughable at first glance," he said. "They wanted to know whether the roofs in a certain village were of thatch or of sheet metal." However, he said, he later learned that the assignment had to do with a particular type of American radar bombsight, in which a village with tin roofs would show up in a characteristic fashion. Wennerström has said that after carrying out this task he informed the General that the Americans were displaying curiosity about tin roofs, obviously as navigational aids. The General was deeply

interested, and, having ordered his people to collect
data on the incidence of sheet-metal roofs in the
Ukraine, he began to plot them on his map in an
attempt to determine just which targets the Americans
might have in mind. Wennerström has said that, after
studying the pattern of metal roofs, the General concluded that because they did not tend to lead to such
things as factory sites, whatever targets the Americans
were aiming at must be spread over the entire Ukraine
and Kuban areas, so what the Americans had in mind
was probably the chance of waging aerial biological
warfare against the harvests in the breadbasket area of
the Soviet Union, using the roofs as navigational mark-
ers.

"Taken together, everything began to show . . . that
the essence of NATO's planning consisted of air strikes
against the Soviet Union, but no invasion," Wennerström testified. The General suggested to him that the
Soviet leaders might find it difficult to accept this
conclusion, because they themselves had a natural
leaning toward land-based strategy. As a result, the
General told him, particularly clear proofs of the
Americans' intentions would have to be provided at
the forthcoming conference. As things turned out,
Wennerström was instrumental in producing just such
proofs. Soon after he had learned of the existence of
the target map at the United States Embassy, he said,
he had told the General about it, and also about his
inability to get a look at it. But one day later on, he
said, he happened to overhear a conversation in which
it was revealed that a copy of this map was to be sent
by courier to American Air Force Headquarters at
Wiesbaden, Germany, and he so informed the General.
The General displayed intense interest, asking for all
sorts of details—who the courier would be, how he
proposed to travel, the time of his departure, and so

on. Wennerström has said that he was able to give the
General all this information. One day about a week
later, according to Wennerström, he was walking to
the Swedish Embassy from his home when he saw the
Soviet contact car pass him and draw up to the curb
a short distance ahead. In accordance with the pre-
scribed procedure in such circumstances, Wennerström ignored the car and walked on to the nearest
telephone booth, from which he dialed the secret number. The voice at the other end told him that arrangements had been made for him to be taken to the
headquarters villa outside Moscow. When Wennerström arrived there, he found the General, who produced a map and asked him if he believed it to be
identical with the one at the American Embassy. Wennerström said, in the light of the target information he
had collected, he thought it was, and when he asked
the General how on earth he had managed to obtain
it, the General told him that, thanks to his information
about the dispatch of the map to Wiesbaden, Soviet
agents had been able to track the courier and at some
point along the route managed to obtain access to it
long enough to photograph it.

Subsequently, Wennerström told his Swedish interrogators, the General "pointed out to the head of
the Soviet Intelligence service that it was thanks to me
that they had been so fortunate," and as a result the
head of the Soviet Intelligence service ordered that
Wennerström be given what the Soviets called "a top
agent's authority," along with the rank of major general in the Soviet Intelligence service. "The title of top
agent means, first of all, that the agent will be given
independent assignments, which he will carry through
to the best of his ability," Wennerström explained after
his arrest. "He will be given no detail work. Secondly,
it means that the agent has full control of funds; thus

it is never necessary to request authority for expenses—for example, if bribes are to be paid to a
certain person, if a trip is to be made, and so on."

Up to the time of the target-map episode, according
to Wennerström, he had received from the Russians,
in addition to the ten thousand rubles turned over to
him by Nikitushev when he was recruited, regular
payment of five thousand rubles a month. Now that
he had acquired the authority to draw funds as he saw
fit, regular payments ceased. Ordinarily, he has said,
he drew sums only as specific needs arose, and the
General made arrangements to deposit regular payments for his espionage activities in an account at the
main headquarters of Soviet Intelligence, where, presumably, Wennerström could come and collect a tidy
amount at some later date. Such escrow arrangements
are common in intelligence work. Wennerström has
said it was understood between him and the General
that "whenever it became necessary in the future I
could reckon on very large payments from the Soviet
side." (Wennerström has indicated his belief that, at
the time of his arrest, his escrow account in Moscow
had a value of "hundreds of thousands of kronor.")

Of his designation as a Soviet major general, Wennerström said he realized that it did not imply a per-
manent position but that it did have "a most important
bearing on the agent's relations with personnel be-
longing to the Soviet Intelligence service." Charac-
teristically, he added the observation that in such a
situation senior rank "makes it possible to go over the
heads of certain persons" within the Soviet Intelligence
organization. Of his work as a whole for the Russians
at this time, he said, "I was left with the very strong
sense of having accomplished something and of having
reached a high level of prestige. And there is no use
denying that thanks to this feeling I experienced a deep

inner satisfaction with the results. I became fascinated with the whole thing, my enthusiasm fanned to some degree by my increasing liking for my Soviet contact man."

Amid these developments, Wennerström told his interrogators, he was simply neglecting Sweden, whose interests he was supposed to be officially representing in Moscow. He insisted that at that time he did not contemplate engaging directly in activities against his own country and that he still considered his delivery of the secret Swedish defense plan to the Russians to have been merely a means of effecting a final penetration of the Soviet Intelligence service. It was true, he admitted, that as far as Swedish interests were concerned, "the edges of the picture became progressively blurred." Certain things he was doing in Moscow might have been illegal from the Swedish point of view, he thought; for example, the Swedish Embassy received reports from the embassies of the NATO countries concerning NATO military matters, and Wennerström read them and "obtained certain information that I used [for Soviet purposes] when it became a question of judging NATO's defense plans." But this sort of thing, he claimed, occurred only on a small scale, and "in the over-all picture" he regarded it as of no consequence. "The longer I continued with my activities, the stronger became my belief that Sweden's role in international relations was completely insignificant," he said. "I knew that various things that I did were not permitted from the Swedish point of view, but I didn't worry my head about it, because they seemed unimportant [compared] with the international activities."

As Wennerström's interest in Swedish matters waned, he became more and more deeply absorbed in the strategic ramifications of the struggle among the

great powers. He testified that, thanks to his increasingly effective relationship with the General and his
own high rank within the Soviet Intelligence service,
the General and he were able to operate under a system
that he understood was seldom used in Soviet Intelligence, owing to a shortage of manpower. The system, the General told him, was known as "pair work,"
and in his case it meant that the General was released
from other assignments so that he and Wennerström
could work as a two-man team to solve intelligence
problems in the fashion they deemed best. Wennerström was, rather naturally, gratified by this arrangement; as far as he himself was concerned, he has said,
the General's "wide experience and background of
knowledge became of significant importance to the
extent that it awakened my interest, carried me along,
and engendered my enthusiasm, all of which was further sharpened by his personal knowledge." Indeed,
this working relationship was so effective that it continued for fourteen years, and if Wennerström had not
been arrested by the Swedes, it would probably have
gone on five years longer, at least.

According to Wennerström, the major Soviet strategic conference for which he had gathered information
concerning NATO military planning and potential
American bombing targets ended with a decision to
give the highest priority to building up Soviet anti-
aircraft defenses. The General told him that in the
effort to strengthen Russia against aerial attack, there
was just one model in the world that was worthy of
being followed—the British air-defense system—and
he urged Wennerström to obtain whatever information
he could about it. He also asked Wennerström to seek
information on the development of American strategic
bombers, on the structure of the Strategic Air Command, on the planning of American air bases from

which attacks could be aimed at the Soviet Union, and on American bombing tactics in general. For information on the British air-defense system, Wennerström sought out the British air attaché and the British Ambassador to Moscow, he has said, and obtained what he could from them, and supplemented this information with material taken from publications he consulted on visits to Stockholm. To obtain information on the Strategic Air Command and on American air bases, he further cultivated officials at the United States Embassy and the embassies of the other NATO countries. He has said that he found it fairly easy to provide his Soviet superiors with new material concerning SAC, because there were large gaps in Soviet Russia's knowledge of the subject.

Meanwhile, in his capacity as a self-styled "independent agent," Wennerström continued to deliver military information about the Soviet Union to the Americans—or so he told his interrogators—even though by now his schedule had grown so crowded that he was using his vacations for this purpose. In the early fifties, he said, he took a vacation with his wife in the Caucasus, staying at Tiflis, Georgia, for the purpose of confirming some information that had been passed to the Americans. The Americans, it seemed, had discovered "through some agent" that a factory between Tiflis and Baku had begun production of a new jet fighter plane, and they had also found out the routes and times of scheduled test flights of the plane. Wennerström's assignment was to travel on a certain day to a point west of Tiflis and observe the plane as it flew overhead, noting the exact time of its passage. Wennerström said he carried out this assignment satisfactorily, and that in return the Americans paid the entire cost of the vacation. He said that all his expenses were paid on a number of other excursions he undertook for the Americans, but apart from this money, and the earlier payment in lire, he received no compensation from the United States, though the transcript of his interrogation hazily describes his receipt of "certain *valuta*" in 1950 or 1951.

Whatever the quantity of military information about the Soviet Union allegedly passed on to the Americans by Wennerström, it was certainly exceeded by the amount of military information about United States military affairs and interests passed on by him to the Soviet Intelligence service. In the course of time, Wennerström has said, there began to grow within him "a significant feeling of loyalty" toward both the General and the Soviet Intelligence service as a whole. The General, for his part, continued his collaboration with Wennerström in a manner that conveyed an increasing confidence in the Swede's ability as a Soviet agent, and he went on with the painstaking briefings in which he filled in details of the strategic considerations related to Wennerström's clandestine activities. According to Wennerström, the Russians' decision to expand their nation's air defenses against nuclear and other bombers was followed by another Soviet strategic conference on air power. At this conference, he said, the Soviet Union's strategic air power was conceded to be far below that of the United States in both quality and quantity. On the one hand, Wennerström said, the American system of air bases clearly made it possible for the United States to launch toward the Soviet Union not only long-range aircraft from the United States but short-range aircraft from forward bases; on the other hand, the Soviet Union, which had no chance of building up a ring of bases around the United States, could depend only on long-range aircraft, for which Russia had no significant construction program at the time. Competition against the United States in this area was therefore considered hopeless, and the Russians decided to give the highest priority to the development of intercontinental rockets with nuclear warheads, which they did not then have. It was also decided, Wennerström said, to develop Soviet strategic aircraft capable of reaching European and Asiatic targets— most notably, American bases on those continents.

At the conclusion of that conference, the General gave Wennerström new instructions for obtaining information that Soviet Intelligence needed in order to fill out its current picture of American air power. Wennerström said that he carried out those instructions as well as he could but that precise technical information was hard to come by. He continued to use his secret telephone number, and also to meet the General according to the prearranged routine. Sometimes, when he stepped into the car with a lengthy report to make, the General would flip a swtich beside his seat, so that the dialogue could be recorded, and, when the information he had was very urgently needed, the General would have a stenographer in the car with him to take notes.

Wennerström still said nothing to the General about any activities, past or present, he might have been engaging in on behalf of the Americans. As a matter of fact, he later told his Swedish interrogators, he was finding it difficult, because of his increasing sympathy toward the Soviet side, to keep up such work. Thus, in 1951, he said, at the request of the American air attaché, he made a trip to the house of a foreign journalist who lived some six miles from a proving ground, outside Moscow, where jet and rocket engines were being tested, to listen to the noises of the tests and deduce what he could from them. He was able to conclude, he said, that one of the engines being tested was that of an ordinary German V-2 rocket, since it

always ran for exactly fifty-five seconds, the normal
burning time for a V-2. On the same occasion, he
heard something else—the sound of a rocket far more
powerful than a V-2, and capable of shaking windows
for miles around. "I came to the conclusion that this
was the first sample of the new Soviet...
intercontinental rocket research," Wennerström has
said. "I thought this was unusually interesting. [But]
my change of sympathies had gone so far that I said
nothing about it to my American contact man."

Conversely, Wennerström was more than ever willing to pass on to the General the observations on military matters made by American officers. The American
military attaché in Moscow in 1951 was Major General
Robert W. Grow, and Wennerström used to see him
fairly often. Wennerström testified that on a number
of occasions he had noticed Grow making notes in a
black pocket memo book. One day, Wennerström's
Soviet superior asked him if it was true that General
Grow was accustomed to carrying such a notebook.
Wennerström said it was. The next thing he heard
about the black notebook was that it had been stolen
while General Grow was on a visit to West Germany,
that it had been photographed and replaced in General
Grow's coat, and that a British Communist writer in
East Germany had used what were purportedly excerpts from a notebook—actually a diary containing
a certain amount of confidential, and even top-secret,
information—to prove that General Grow was an
American warmonger engaged in espionage against the
Soviet Union. (General Grow was later court-martialed
on charges that included the improper recording of
classified information in private records, and was con-
victed and sentenced to a six-month suspension from
command. The black diary was real, all right, but, as

a thorough United States Army investigation determined, the purported excerpts containing warmongering remarks weren't. They were Soviet distortions.)

According to Wennerström, his interest in working for the Soviet Intelligence service now began to overshadow entirely the work that he was supposedly doing for the Americans. During his pre-trial interrogation in Sweden, he attempted to explain the development of his attitudes toward the Soviet Union in these words:

When I first jumped into international espionage among the big powers, I had a feeling of sympathy for NATO and an antipathy for the Soviet Union. It so happened, however, that during my stay in Moscow there was a progressive change in my sympathies, which ended up by their swinging completely to the other side. What I have said may be incomprehensible . . . but I cannot do otherwise than relate how things actually developed. A strong supplementary reason was that I had a chance to see behind the scenes on both sides. It was entirely obvious that the Soviet Intelligence efforts were of a defensive nature and that those of the Americans were offensive.

If I had fulfilled my original intentions . . . then I would have, so to speak, delivered my Soviet contact man to my American one. Such a thing became very quickly repulsive to me. So the consequence was that I became an agent for both sides.

As a result of the concatenation of events and the undoubtedly great influence that the Soviet General's personality had on me, I came to feel myself more and more a trusted member of a powerful organization. To this must be added the fact that I had been fortunate in my activities in a way which had not corresponded to anything that I had intended to undertake in the course of my life.

The transformation in my attitude went a step further,

I might say, to the point that I looked on my work with the Americans as an excellent way to achieve better results for the Soviet Intelligence service.

Whatever other activities Wennerström engaged in during his service in Moscow, he seems to have carried out his legitimate work as Swedish air attaché to the satisfaction of his superiors in Stockholm. During one of his trips home, he told Major General Gustaf Adolf Westring, Chief of the Swedish Air Force Staff, that he "was very happy with my Moscow assignment and was not at all averse to having it extended several years." At the same time, he let General Westring know that he would not be averse to a future assignment in London or Washington—preferably Washington. Some time after this conversation, the Swedish air attaché in Washington happened to become ill, and at the beginning of 1952 General Westring wrote to Wennerström formally offering him the assignment, beginning that April. Wennerström accepted, and informed his Soviet contact man of his impending transfer. "This came as a complete surprise to him and his superior, and their reaction was somewhat as though they had won the big prize in a lottery," Wennerström has remarked. In Washington, as an agent "in place"—that is, a qualified and cleared insider, rather than a clandestine operative, or "illegal"—his usefulness would presumably be even greater.

In Wennerström's remaining weeks in Moscow, he was given detailed briefings on the activities he was expected to carry out for the Russians in Washington. Midway through this series of briefings, however, he received a terrible shock: the Russians told him that they had discovered his connection with the Americans. According to his account, this had occurred not through any lack of caution on his part but because of carelessness on the American side. It had been impressed upon him, as it was on all Soviet Intelligence officers, that the real name of an agent was never to be used in a report, and it seemed that the Americans had broken this rule, using his name in a coded message sent out over the radio transmitter in the American Embassy in Moscow; Soviet Intelligence, which routinely monitored such transmissions, was able to decipher the broadcast. "The radio message in question referred to certain information I had furnished [the Americans] upon my return from certain trips. After the Soviets had made a check, they had no doubt at all about my being a double agent [for the Americans]," Wennerström has said.

Wennerström was told of this discovery at one of the meetings in the villa. "My first reaction was one of unspeakable bitterness against the Americans for not being able to protect themselves better," Wennerström recalled. He testified that he had no idea what to do or say when he was confronted with this information. He remembered that he had thought it strange, when the meeting began, that the General had four people with him, including a man who was introduced as the General's superior officer and another whom Wennerström recognized, from their previous encounter, as the man responsible for surveillance of foreign diplomats in Moscow. "The first thought that went through my mind was that it was very possible they were going to liquidate me with a shot in the nape of the neck. We were a long distance from Moscow, and nobody knew where I was," Wennerström said. But, he went on, it turned out that he was mistaken about the Soviet reaction. "I don't know what happened between the General and his superior before our meeting. One thing stood out clearly, however, and that was that my contact man was heart and soul on my side. There was not a single word from the Soviets of reproach. . . . The Soviet General had thought about my situation before, and he and several of his superiors had wondered many times how I could possibly obtain the information I did from the Americans. He said now, 'Here is the explanation of your success.' "

According to his account of the meeting, Wennerström assured the General that by this time no one could have any doubt about where his, Wennerström's, true sympathies lay. The General then explained to him "that if the discovery had occurred at a considerably earlier stage, it could have had consequences that there was no use in even talking about now." But, the General said, as things stood, it was a tremendous advantage for the Soviets to have contacts in United States Intelligence circles, and it was the desire of the Soviets, looking toward Wennerström's appointment in Washington, that he continue his relations with the Americans as though no change had taken place, and that, if possible, he make the contacts even more intimate. At the same time, Wennerström has said, the General obtained from him details of his work on behalf of the Americans in the Soviet Union, and they came to an understanding about the reporting of his future dealing with American Intelligence.

Understandably, Wennerström was enormously relieved at this outcome of the confrontation. At that point, he has said, "from my side the swing to the Soviet side was complete and definitive. . . . Instead of being a false agent inside of Soviet Intelligence, I was now this same thing within the American organization." As he later put it, "My truly great opportunities did not open up until I went to Washington."

Three

W<small>HEN</small>, IN APRIL 1952, WENNERSTRÖM ARRIVED IN Washington to take up his post as air attaché at the Swedish Embassy, he could hardly have been made more generally welcome by American officials. So far as they were concerned, he was the military representative of a highly civilized, technically advanced nation—one that, even if it remained militarily neutral in the Cold War, was unquestionably friendly to the democratic cause. According to the reputation that preceded him to this country, Wennerström was one of the more pro-American members of the Swedish diplomatic corps. And he was additionally welcome owing to his reputation of being something of a Soviet expert. In fact, according to one Pentagon source, during visits to Stockholm from Moscow prior to his departure for Washington Wennerström was "treated as a celebrity at the American Embassy." Indeed, some of the diplomatic personnel there are said to have behaved "like a bunch of cub reporters" in soliciting his opinions on Soviet affairs.

All things considered, Colonel Wennerström seemed a very desirable addition to the Washington diplomatic corps, and various people did their best to help him get settled in the capital. An American officer who had known him in Moscow arranged for a house to be rented to the Colonel—who was accompanied by his wife and their two daughters—and also went to the trouble of reserving a place in a suitable private school for the younger Wennerström girl. In addition, the American officer, who owned two cars, offered Wennerström the use of one until he had a chance to buy his own. Everybody in Washington seemed to find Wennerström agreeable. He was tall, slim, blond and blue-eyed, and in spite of partial baldness he was, at forty-six, a man of unusually handsome appearance. One United States Air Force officer has recalled, "He was very gracious and polished, with a certain air of reserve about him. His English was fluent. He was the sort of man people would look at twice." Nearly everybody, of course, was interested in the Colonel's experiences in the Soviet Union, and among those interested were some Intelligence officers in the Pentagon, who made contact with him not long after his arrival and asked for his appraisal of various aspects of Russian air power. Wennerström apparently responded to their queries in a friendly and professional fashion, but, whatever he may have told them about the Soviet Union, he certainly neglected to inform them of his interesting connections with the Soviet Intelligence service.

The espionage tasks that Wennerström was to carry out in Washington had of course been the subject of long discussions with the General in the special Soviet Intelligence briefings before Wennerström had left

Moscow. As Wennerström later recalled these talks, their main theme was the effort of the Soviet Union to attain a political, military, and technological balance of power with the United States and the NATO bloc, by whose forces the Soviet Union felt itself mortally threatened. To help the Russians form a realistic picture of United States air strength, Wennerström was to pass on whatever material he could get concerning the latest American developments in bombers, fighters, guided missiles, bombsights, radar, high-frequency radio, and advanced photographic-reconnaissance equipment. He was told not to bother with such "unnecessary" intelligence as data on the organization and personnel of the Defense Department—matters that he was given to understand were being taken care of by "an agent or agents" within the Pentagon. Even in his own field of military aviation, he was not required, as a general thing, to report on just what planes were stationed at particular Air Force bases in the United States, because, he was told, such information was already being adequately reported. According to Wennerström, the General told him that his local Soviet contact man in Washington would be the Soviet air attaché; Wennerström was given passwords to be used at their first meeting. Beyond that, Wennerström had no precise instructions, because, as he later explained it, his position as a top agent would enable him to make for himself whatever arrangements he considered best. As for the General, he had told Wennerström that he would continue to work with him from Moscow, their primary means of communication being microfilmed messages and material.

The principal function of an air attaché is to act as an official observer of the strength and development of the air force of the country to which he is accredited. He is, technically, an Intelligence officer, but he is expected to confine himself to overt and legal means of gathering information. In Washington, diplomatic usage requires him to channel his queries through a section of the Pentagon known as Foreign Liaison, which is supposed to see to it that whatever information is given out cannot endanger the national security. All requests by an attaché to visit Air Force installations or defense plants must also be cleared through this office. As might be expected, what an attaché is officially allowed to learn depends largely on the relations between his own government and the United States, and Wennerström benefited from his government's excellent standing with Pentagon officials. Aeronautical data were made even more accessible to him because of the fact that, in addition to his other duties, he was head of the United States Purchasing Commission for the Swedish Air Force. When he arrived in Washington, the Swedish Air Force was not a notably big buyer of American matériel, but later, as Sweden began to strengthen her air-defense system, the situation changed considerably. The Swedish Air Force constantly required a vast amount of highly technical information, and to provide this Wennerström turned to his contacts within the Pentagon, where, according to a Swedish colleague of his at the time, "all doors stood open to him." As head of the Purchasing Commission, Wennerström was also supposed to pay visits to aircraft and electronics plants, and here, too, he was made thoroughly welcome.

Altogether, he had an almost perfect cover for espionage activities. In making what he did of his opportunities—so he eventually told his interrogators—he kept in mind some advice that, he said, a Swedish general had given him about making and maintaining contacts in the United States. To quote Wennerström's interrogation transcript, "He [the general] pointed out

[that] it is necessary, in most cases, to include the women. He said that [American] women had a much greater influence over the men than we realize. If a closer contact with somebody is desired and if the spouse of the party concerned could be interested in the meetings, she would be a driving factor to a great extent.... I found out that his observations were completely correct."

Wennerström's first contact with the Soviet Intelligence service in Washington came when, shortly after his arrival, he paid introductory visits, according to protocol, to the air attachés at various embassies. The Soviet air attaché at the time was Major General Viktor Kuvinov, and Wennerström, when he called on him at the Soviet Embassy, expected to exchange with him the passwords agreed upon in Moscow. "He would tell me that an acquaintance in Moscow had asked to be remembered to me—a man called Nikolai Vasilyevich," Wennerström later told his interrogators in Sweden. "And in reply I would thank him and say that I knew the person very well, and that I remembered having met him several times at a place in Moscow called Spiridonovka." But Kuvinov failed to utter the password, and after a friendly and inconsequential chat Wennerström took his leave. In August, Kuvinov paid a return visit to Wennerström at his office, and this time the agreed-upon words were exchanged. Wennerström, thinking himself able to talk safely, began to bring up with the Soviet attaché what he later referred to as "special problems," but Kuvinov at once clapped a hand over Wennerström's mouth so hard as almost to bruise him and, without saying anything, showed him a note suggesting a further meeting in an office not far from the Swedish Embassy.

At this next meeting, Wennerström was handed five

thousand dollars in United States currency—an amount
that Wennerström, before his departure from Moscow,
had arranged to draw for what he subsequently described as "starting capital" for his espionage work in
this country. He was also given a schedule for regular
meetings in secluded places in Washington—the exact
spots have not been made public up to now by either
the Swedes or the Americans—so that material representing the fruits of Wennerström's espionage could
be transferred. Both for this purpose and for his legitimate duties, Wennerström had already installed in
a closet in his office a Leica camera mounted on a
stand, with accessories that permitted the photographing of documents at close range.

Wennerström now set to work supplying Soviet Intelligence with the sort of information it wanted. "The
possibilities of obtaining publications were almost fantastic," he said later. For the most part, he procured
these simply by writing to the Pentagon, in his capacity
as Swedish air attaché, and asking for them. "From
this great volume of literature I selected the material
that was suitable for my purposes on the basis of the
aims of the Soviet Intelligence service, and I sent such
material both to Sweden and to Moscow," he said. "I
went on trips within the United States and Canada on
all imaginable occasions, to aircraft units and the aircraft industries.... Some of these trips were official
trips for Sweden but many had a different purpose.
My lively contacts with the American Air Force re-
sulted in an acquaintance with persons at, or in rec-
ommendations to, practically every place I went.... I
had entrée everywhere."

Since American manufacturers of military aircraft,
with the Korean War nearing an end, were begging
for orders, and since Sweden was known as a customer
able to pay cash in dollars for whatever it bought, it

is reasonable to assume that Wennerström was an extraordinarily welcome visitor to defense plants. Speak-
ing of his relations with sales executives of such
companies, Wennerström has remarked, "My interest
in data [for espionage purposes] and their interest in
a sale met at the same level. . . . I can say that many
times very astonishing results were obtained." As time
went on, Sweden made larger and larger purchases of
military aircraft and other equipment in this country,
and this did nothing to injure Wennerström's standing.
He has said that in dealing with an aircraft company
he would first make contact with sales executives, and
then, through them, would "foster relations" with the
top men in the company, who would usually, as he
said, "express themselves in a positive way" about
him, indicating to underlings that he was a man whom
it was useful to help. Wennerström recalled that once,
when he was talking with a sales executive at a large
industrial plant in the Los Angeles area, the sales executive telephoned the head of the company and told
him of Wennerström's presence, whereupon the boss
invited both Wennerström and the executive to join
him that afternoon at his private swimming pool. "In
America, such a little thing as this makes such a tremendous impression on a subordinate official that it
can be utilized in a very efficient way," Wennerström
said later.

One of his ways of using such contacts, according
to Wennerström, was to show interest in equipment
that he knew he would never buy for Sweden but that
he also knew would be of interest to the Soviets. By
thus taking advantage of opportunities "to go side-
wise," as he has put it, he was able to pick up a good
deal of useful intelligence. He has also said that on
various occasions he resorted to outright bribery to
obtain information for Soviet Intelligence; in the United

States, he told his Swedish interrogators, it was a very simple matter to buy information. References to bribery show up a number of times in the heavily censored transcript of his pre-trial interrogation. At one point, describing his stay in the United States, he said, "Through some of my connections with the electronics companies I was able to gradually get this information on——and I think that I paid one thousand dollars for it. It was sent to the Soviet Union." At another point, he is quoted as saying, "I was also given a complete description of the design of——. They went only to Moscow. . . . I got them the bribing way on the spot." By one means or another, Wennerström collected and transmitted to the Soviets what has been described as "a huge amount" of written material from defense plants, including tables of organization and lists of key personnel—items that were useful to Soviet Intelligence, Wennerström said, when it came to recruiting agents.

In addition to his own trips to defense factories, Wennerström had the responsibility of arranging visits by other Swedes who were concerned with military aviation. Whether or not he accompanied these people on their visits, he usually managed to talk with them later about what they had learned, and he also arranged to be supplied with copies of the reports they sent back to Sweden. The visitors included specialists in radar, atomic energy, and guided missiles, and Wennerström told his interrogators that whenever, in his opinion, their reports contained information of special value to the Russians, he conveyed the contents to Soviet Intelligence. The documents that Wennerström considered of particular use to the Russians in most cases he photographed with the Leica in the evenings or on weekends. So that he could do his photography without interruption, he installed a red light outside the door of his office, and gave his secretary orders not to enter or allow anyone else to enter while the light was on. In any event, nobody was likely to be suspicious, he said, explaining, "If, against my expectations, somebody should disregard the red lamp and come in, I could always say that the photographic work had to do with material we were supposed to send to Sweden." Because Wennerström's legitimate work for Sweden involved the photographing of unclassified documents emanating from the Pentagon, and because he often photographed the same documents for the Russians, he was under "constant pressure," he recalled, to insure that he didn't get his documents or films mixed up and send them to the wrong clients. As a consequence, he was particularly careful to perform his photographic work in a very concentrated and systematic way.

In his photography, Wennerström used two types of 35-millimeter film. One, a conventional type, was for material that he thought could be traced back to him only with great difficulty. The other, he told his interrogators, was a secretly formulated film provided by his Soviet contact man in Washington. This film could be successfully developed only in Moscow, and ordinary developing chemicals would automatically erase any latent image on it. This type of film was for photographing documents that could be more easily traced to Wennerström.

When he had to hand over only small quantities of film, he would do so by shaking hands with his contact man in some public place—in a department store, say, or on the street. When it was done on the street, Wennerström and the other man would approach each other from opposite directions, and "one would look surprised and one would shake hands and nod and continue on one's way." They also transferred film at

diplomatic gatherings, usually managing to meet in
the most crowded part of a room. On one occasion,
Wennerström testified, he delivered film to his Soviet
contact right in the Pentagon during an official meeting
there, and he also has spoken of passing film "in the
middle of a room and right under the noses of high-
ranking American officers." Wennerström has said that
to master this handshaking technique he and his Soviet
contact had "started with exercises on a large scale"
shortly after he arrived in Washington. He said that
these practice sessions did not imply any lack of dex-
terity on his own part. "That was more because he
[Kuvinov] couldn't do it than because I couldn't," he
said. Some transfers were made during plane trips and
some were made during receptions at the Russian Embassy. Wennerström would leave film in an inner pocket
of his topcoat, which he would check at the cloakroom
upon his arrival. Then, during the reception, he would
murmur to his Soviet contact the number of his cloakroom check. The contact man would thereupon go to
the cloakroom, remove the film, return to the reception, and give Wennerström a slight nod to indicate
that the transfer had been made.

According to Wennerström, these were not the only
espionage transactions that he engaged in at the Soviet
Embassy. He told his interrogators that because of his
standing with the Americans, and because of the American Intelligence contacts he had made in both Moscow
and Washington, he was put in touch, sometime after
his arrival in Washington, with representatives of the
Central Intelligence Agency. He said that his contact
with the C.I.A. began with a lunch in the Pentagon
that was attended, apparently by design of his hosts,
by a C.I.A. man. After the lunch, he said, the C.I.A.
man took him aside and told him that "he knew that
I had rendered [the Americans] much valuable help."

He mentioned then that he had something of interest to discuss with me if I had time that afternoon and was willing. I was first afraid that they had detected some of my [espionage] activity in the United States. . . . I accepted his invitation. . . . We went in his private car to an out-of-the-way office in Washington with no door plates. It turned out during the trip that he was apparently not a native of Washington because he had a hard time finding the place. . . . The person in question, who I presume had a false name, asked me whether I was willing to help them over some difficulties they had. My reaction was one of relief, because it was not as I had feared— that they had found out about my activity—and I answered "yes." He explained that there was material in the Soviet Embassy that had to be gotten out of there. He then asked me to what extent I was invited to the Soviet Embassy and apparently found my answer satisfactory.

As a result of this and other contacts with C.I.A. people, Wennerström said, he agreed to attend functions at the Soviet Embassy regularly so that, at a suitable time, he would be on hand to receive there, from a Russian-speaking contact who would make himself known in an exchange of passwords, a small package, which Wennerström was to pass on to a C.I.A. agent at a meeting place in Washington. Wennerström has said that he subsequently completed two such missions in the Soviet Embassy on behalf of the C.I.A., and that he was given a thousand dollars each time for doing so. After that, he had no further contact with the C.I.A., he told his interrogators.

On behalf of Soviet Intelligence, Wennerström has said, he photographed so much material that on many occasions it was impossible for him to transfer the exposed film by the usual means. To transfer material in bulk, he and his contact would meet in some isolated

place—perhaps in a park or on a deserted street—
usually after dark. Because of the activities of the
Federal Bureau of Investigation and other security
agencies, according to Wennerström, his contact would
have to be on the move around Washington for between two and five hours ahead of the time agreed on
for the meeting, in order to shake off possible shadows.
Some indication of the complexity of these evasive
maneuvers can be gathered from a Swedish security
police account of a talk Wennerström remembered
having with the General about similar precautions taken
by Russians in Stockholm:

> The General told Colonel Wennerström that . . . if an
> employee of the [Soviet] Embassy went out to meet [a
> Soviet agent] they might order a man to go out to attract
> members of the security police. This man would be a
> member of the Intelligence service, and he would then
> attract the members of the security police to himself.
> This man would act as if he were on some important
> assignment, but at all times he had to be careful not to
> lose the security men who were following him. After a
> while one more man would be sent out from the Embassy.
> He would act in the same manner, to attract other per-
> sonnel from the security police who might be in the
> vicinity. The person who would make the actual contact
> [with the agent] would be the third person sent out of
> the Embassy, and it would be assumed that no more
> security police would be available to follow him. How-
> ever, should this ruse fail, the third man would attempt
> to shake the security police off.

Wennerström himself did not undertake elaborate
maneuvers to elude detection; he told his interrogators
that he believed himself to be watched very little, if
at all, in Washington, partly because he was a neutral

and partly because American counter-intelligence manpower was overtaxed by keeping track of the diplomatic corps as a whole. When Wennerström and his Soviet contact approached a meeting place, however, they did use a signaling system to indicate the presence or absence of danger. Wennerström later explained it by saying, "One should always have the left hand freely moving back and forth when walking. If there was anything to carry, it was done with the right hand. When it was believed that danger was imminent, the left hand was put into the pocket of the trousers or topcoat. . . . As soon as one put the hand into the pocket, the contact man was to act as if he did not know the counterpart at all."

Sometimes, if Wennerström had films ready for delivery and his contact considered a meeting inadvisable, they had recourse to a letter-cache system, or, as it is known in the espionage trade, a "dead drop." In a dead drop, one man leaves the material in a certain spot and the other later picks it up, according to a prearranged schedule; thus the sender and receiver avoid the risk entailed in making a transfer during a personal encounter, or "live drop." The details of the letter-cache system that Wennerström used have not been revealed, possibly for security reasons, but it is likely that it involved his communicating with his contact man by means of chalk marks or some similar method, for, according to people who are informed on the subject, apparently simple signs of this kind are often used by professionals to convey quite elaborate instructions.

On certain occasions, when Wennerström was to deliver bulk material in person, he met his contact not in Washington but somewhere in the countryside nearby. The Soviet air attaché liked to fish, Wennerström has revealed, and, on at least one occasion, received his Swedish agent on the banks of a stream

near Washington; there they sat down on the grass and
enjoyed a picnic lunch that the Russian had brought
along while Wennerström reported on his recent activities and handed over his films in a leisurely way.
(The Soviet attaché was careful not to be caught fishing
illegally; according to Wennerström, he had taken out
an angling license, and had brought it with him on this
day.) At a meeting like this, Wennerström would hand
over very considerable amounts of microfilm—between fifteen and twenty-five rolls, or even more. Once,
he said, he handed over about a hundred and fifty
rolls—which could have contained as many as five
thousand exposures. Film bearing material that he considered routine he carried in a brown paper bag; if the
material was urgent, he used a white paper bag. In
return for the exposed film, he received a supply of
new special film, and from time to time, as he requested it, he received money, in amounts ranging
from a thousand to four thousand dollars. Part of this,
he testified, was used for bribing people in defense
plants "and other expenses."

Sometimes, by means of special signaling systems,
the contact man scheduled an emergency meeting in
order to get instructions to Wennerström. One day,
for example, Wennerström testified, he was accosted
by his Soviet friend "in a precipitate manner" and told
that a high-priority message had been received from
Moscow asking that he check on a report that the
United States was preparing a "surprise action" against
the Soviet Union. Wennerström proceeded on the theory, he said, that if some sudden attack against the
Soviet Union was indeed being prepared, there would
be frantic activity in the Pentagon, so he drove over
there and called on the aides of various high officers,
to see whether he could make appointments with their
superiors in the very near future. There seemed to be

no difficulty about making the appointments, and, after several further inquiries, he left. "I drew my own conclusions," Wennerström said, "and . . . in the afternoon of the same day I reported that according to my judgment the reports received by Moscow . . . were definitely false." Thereafter, he testified, he was relied upon by Soviet Intelligence in times of crisis as an especially good source of information that would help avoid miscalculations of the kind that might lead to war by accident.

Thus, during the Suez crisis in 1956, Wennerström has said, he sent a report concerning the movements of American air units in the Mediterranean. With his customary efficiency, he also got off a cable to his superiors in Stockholm containing this information. He later told the Swedish security police that the Russians attached particular value to his report because it arrived in Moscow three days before the events he referred to took place. Being able to make such contributions, he said, gave a "greater depth" to his political thinking, and during his service in Washington he became increasingly aware of the importance of espionage as a means of preserving peace. Whatever thoughts Wennerström had in this direction certainly must have been reinforced during two home leaves, at the end of 1953 and in the summer of 1955, for on both occasions he made surreptitious trips to Finland, where, following very detailed instructions given well in advance, he met with the General, in great secrecy, at night in a villa outside Helsinki. ("In Moscow they had apparently been so well informed that they even knew what clothes I had. For these meetings I was instructed to wear a certain hat and a certain coat.") According to Wennerström, the talks the two men held were accompanied from first to last by very loud radio music. As one subject after another was dealt with,

an aide of the General's marked off item after item on
a list before him, and Wennerström did the same thing
with notes of his own. At the conclusion of each ses-
sion, all the papers that had been used were burned,
and ordinarily the ashes were flushed down a toilet.
Then Wennerström, the General, and the aide would
move into another room, where a good meal would
be served, and in the middle of the meal the General
would produce still another paper and put it on a plate
near Wennerström. "On this paper were a number of
points for the discussion of general political, military,
or strategic problems," Wennerström said. "As soon
as we had gone over these points, he marked them off.
After this, there was, of course, also conversation . . .
intended to clarify my views on certain situations in
the world. . . . These talks [also] made it possible to
obtain a clear picture of Russian views." At these
secret meetings, it appears, Wennerström's respect for
and friendship with the General remained undimin-
ished, and he seems to have felt that the General had
as high a regard for him, both professionally and personally, as ever. Wennerström has said that during one
of these visits the General had him fill out an application for Soviet citizenship, which meant that if he
had managed to leave Sweden before his arrest the
Soviet government would have automatically given
him refuge.

In Washington, from the beginning to the end of
his service there, Wennerström was not under the
slightest suspicion from either the Americans or his
Swedish colleagues. According to several of the Swedes
who worked with him, his espionage was so thoroughly masked by his legitimate work that any traces
of it would have been extremely difficult to detect even
if he had been under suspicion. And his standing in

the diplomatic community rendered him even less liable to vigilance. "From what everybody here seemed to think, he was very hard-working, very dedicated," an American officer in the Pentagon has said of him. Carl Fredrik Schnell, who is now a lieutenant colonel in the Swedish Air Force, and who, as a major, served under Wennerström in Washington for two years or so as assistant Swedish air attaché, later said that in those days he regarded Wennerström as highly efficient at his official duties. "Thousands of questions were always coming at us from the Swedish Air Force concerning ... complex matters about aerodynamics, ballistics, and so on. Wennerström always seemed to be able to get the questions answered," Schnell has observed, "Although he wasn't a technician, he had a certain feel for what was valuable information, and he knew where to look for it. ... He was always very thorough, very systematic. Everything always was in very good order. He never liked to ask for more than one copy of a technical document. ... He would say to me, 'We're guests in this country—don't burden the host government. Let them photograph the material in Stockholm, and then Stockholm can give us extra copies.' He almost never sent a document to Sweden without asking for a copy of it from Stockholm. I thought that very efficient. And he seemed to be very security-minded about his Swedish work. I often saw him take a document or some jotting on military matters that he'd finished with and burn it in a large ashtray on his desk, and then he would take the ashes out to a toilet and flush them down. I thought that was an example of how a military attaché in a foreign country should behave where security was concerned. His manner was always very correct. He would always impress upon his wife and upon me that we must never violate traffic laws in a country where we were guests.

He was very strict about this, and when his wife got a parking ticket he always forced her immediately to pay the fine, even though, as an attaché's wife, she had diplomatic immunity. He paid great attention to socializing with important people. He was socially ambitious, there is no doubt about that. Apart from the partygoing, he didn't seem to have any outside interests, and, with his work load, I don't suppose I would have had time for any, either. He was often at the office very early in the mornings, and often, too, he would be there in the evenings and on weekends."

Schnell also recalled that he found Wennerström an unfailingly courteous and considerate superior, who would always go out of his way to help someone faced with a professional or personal difficulty. The two officers lunched together almost every day at a small, rather run-down restaurant on Connecticut Avenue, which, according to Schnell, nobody else at the Embassy "would dream of going to." Sometimes, on the way to lunch, Wennerström would talk to Schnell about his previous assignment in Moscow: "He said that it was awful, because you could never talk freely, and that even the servants at the Embassy and at his residence were Soviet agents. He told me that when he and his wife wanted to talk privately they had to go to a park to do so." Occasionally, Wennerström would engage in very general discussions of the world situation, but, according to Schnell, he stuck to factual matters and tended to back away from "deeper" discussions. "There were no whys or hows in his conversation," Schnell said. "Most people seemed to find him charming, but my wife used to say to me, 'I think Stig is the dullest person I know.' She didn't think he was charming. She had more the impression of coldness."

Another fellow-officer of Wennerström's, who knew

him for more than thirty years, has made the interesting observation that Wennerström, for all his outward grace, lacked what he called "touchable affection"— a quality that the officer defined as the kind of relationship with other people that enables a man, who, for instance, is taking a friend aside, to guide him gently by an elbow or shoulder. "Except for handshakes, I never saw Wennerström touch a person— the arm of an old friend, the arm of a lady getting up from table at a dinner party," this officer said.

At the shabby restaurant on Connecticut Avenue, Schnell recalls, Wennerström would nearly always have the same lunch—ham and eggs, a cup of coffee, and a roll, for which he paid seventy-five cents, leaving the waiter a ten-cent tip. Schnell says that he has often wondered of late whether the restuarant was one of the places where Wennerström left espionage material for his Soviet contact, but he has concluded that by lunching there regularly Wennerström was making the point that he didn't have money to throw around. In Washington, Wennerström lived reasonably well but by no means extravagantly. He later estimated that his income from the Swedish government was about fifteen hundred dollars a month after taxes and other deductions. As for the money he received in Washington from Soviet Intelligence, he said that it averaged out at about seven hundred and fifty dollars a month— tax-free, of course. But he added that out of this he had substantial expenses, such as bribes, to pay, and that he actually drew very little for himself, first, because he was careful never to let money from Soviet Intelligence show up in any bank account or other business record, and, second, because "I had agreed with headquarters in Moscow that I could take out a very high amount [when] I deemed the situation to be favorable." In all, during his service in the United

States he had a tidy sum put away for him regularly in a postal-savings account that the Swedish Defense Staff maintained for him; he deposited further sums in a regular account with a Washington bank; and he had been told that credits were piling up for him in an escrow account in Moscow.

Altogether, in his more than five years of service in Washington, Wennerström probably supplied Soviet Intelligence with film bearing tens of thousands of exposures, with each frame of film reproducing one, or occasionally two, pages of documents or drawings. According to his testimony, this material included, among other things, "data on how new nuclear weapons should be used and the effect expected"; information about bombsights used on strategic bombers; and a report by Wennerström on a visit he paid to a base of the Strategic Air Command, where, according to Schnell, he inspected "everything," even areas to which entry was forbidden to all but a few United States Air Force people. Wennerström's most important acts of espionage for Soviet Intelligence were carried out in the last year or so of his Washington service, having been initiated after the Swedish Air Force had expressed interest in buying two types of United States missiles—the ground-to-air Bomarc and the air-to-ground HM-55. Wennerström obtained highly detailed plans of these weapons and elaborate data concerning their performance, and, in addition to sending this on to Stockholm, he turned most of it over to Soviet Intelligence. (Later, in Sweden, he obtained still more information on these weapons.) Some idea of the scope of this project may be gathered from an estimate by people in the Pentagon that Wennerström would have had to spend some thirty hours "of good hard work" to copy the documents pertaining to one missile. And every page he photographed contained highly classified information.

Four

WENNERSTRÖM'S TOUR OF DUTY IN WASHINGTON
ended in June of 1957, and his many American military
acquaintances seem to have been sorry to see him go.
Upon his departure for Sweden, he took with him not
only their best wishes but also an American decoration,
the Order of the Legion of Merit, which had been
awarded him in recognition of his services as a diplomat friendly to the American cause. The Swedes,
too, seem to have been pleased with his work. Before
he left Washington, his superiors in Stockholm offered
him the post of air attaché in London, but, by his own
account, though he felt attracted to the idea, he had
doubts about taking the job—not because his Soviet
employers had any objections, but for personal reasons. For one thing, he said, if he were to live in
London for some years, his children would grow up
having had no schooling whatever in Sweden. Then,
too, he had to consider that, as a regular officer in the

Swedish Air Force, he had only four more years to go before reaching the mandatory retirement age of fifty-five, and he indicated to his interrogators that, beyond his legitimate military career and his illegitimate espionage career, he wanted to prepare the way for a third career, perhaps a commercial one, which he could pursue in Sweden after his retirement. So, after thinking matters over, he turned the London offer down in favor of a post in Stockholm—that of head of the Air Section of the Command Office of the Swedish Defense Ministry—a position that, among other things, made him chief liaison officer between the Defense Ministry and the air attachés of foreign embassies in Stockholm. This, Wennerström said, looked like a "quiet and pleasant" job, and he was pleased because in it "I could keep up my acquaintance with the diplomatic corps, which both my wife and I greatly enjoyed." It also had another advantage: it provided very effective camouflage for contacts with the Soviet Embassy.

Wennerström took up his new post in October 1957. In December of that year, he made a third visit to Helsinki to meet his friend the General, and explained to him in detail the nature of his new work. Wennerström has said that the General expressed no great interest in Swedish affairs, saying he did not want Wennerström to engage in any activity "not of direct significance concerning his [the General's] sector of operations, namely the U.S.A. and NATO." What did concern the General about Sweden, he said, was the inability of the Soviets to allay an increasing suspicion that behind the screen of its official policy of strict neutrality Sweden was secretly developing close military relations with the United States. The General said that in particular the Russians suspected the existence of a secret link between the Swedish Defense Operations Staff and American Air Force headquarters in Germany. The General asked Wennerström to keep him informed about any deviation from Sweden's official position of neutrality, about visits of American military-aviation experts to Sweden and vice versa, and about the shipment to Sweden of war matériel from the United States, including nuclear weapons, if any. Wennerström's espionage contact in Stockholm, the General said, was to be the Soviet air attaché, Colonel Semyon Ushenko (who later called on Wennerström, gave him the passwords, and handed him an initial payment of ten thousand kronor—about two thousand dollars).

Eventually Wennerström provided himself with a supplementary means of communication with Soviet Intelligence in the form of a powerful short-wave radio set, which, he testified, he obtained as a result of a meeting with the General in East Berlin in March 1958. The preparations for this meeting began in Helsinki at the end of 1957, when Wennerström let the General know that a man he later described as "one of my closest American friends," a general in the American Air Force in Germany, had invited Wennerström and his wife to visit him at Wiesbaden. Wennerström said he had asked the General if he had any special requests in connection with the visit. The General replied that he had, and that Wennerström should keep the date open. Soon, Wennerström testified, he was asked by Moscow to arrange it for a particular time in March 1958, to stay as physically close to the American and his family as possible, and, afterward, to report to a contact in East Berlin. Wennerström told the Swedish security police:

> On the next to the last day of our visit, the [American] general left in a hurry for Turkey. When we left, he had

not yet returned. We left Wiesbaden for Berlin, staying at the Hotel Kempinski. West Berlin was nice for shopping and such things. I was able to arrange for my wife to be shopping while I was in East Berlin. At that time it was possible to move freely between East Berlin and West Berlin. According to my instructions, I was to go by a certain subway train departing from West Berlin at a certain time, get off at a certain station in East Berlin, leave the station and cross a square to a motion-picture theatre and look at the posters. At a distance, I saw another person on the other side of the street. When he saw me, he moved toward the theatre. The man proved to be the same contact [used in effecting Wennerström's meetings with the General in Helsinki, the kind of intermediary known in the trade as a "cutout"]. We went around the corner, where a car was waiting. The car took us to a villa where [the General was waiting and where] a meal had been prepared. The General was particularly anxious, and the first thing he asked me was "How did things go in Wiesbaden?" I reported that we had stayed with the family and that nothing at all had happened, except that the American general had taken off by air in a hurry. "Where to? Where to? This is of very great importance." "Turkey," I replied. He immediately left the room, obviously to send a telegram to Moscow. Through subsequent events I learned that the visit of the American general to Turkey was connected with the reconnoitering of airfields for American paratroopers later committed in connection with the Lebanon crisis.

After a while, the General rejoined Wennerström, saying that nobody knew whether or not a war would break out as time went on, and that it was necessary to prepare for the future. According to Wennerström, the General then asked him, "Are you willing to continue your work, no matter what happens?" Wennerström replied that he was, whereupon the General said,

"If anything of a political nature happens that causes our contact with you to be completely broken, you must do nothing. Even if years pass, you must only wait for a contact. The same contact procedure, with greetings from Nikolai Vasilyevich, will be used." Wennerström testified that the General went on to tell him to buy a short-wave radio on which he could receive coded messages from the Soviet Union. Wennerström was given a listening schedule, a list of frequencies to tune in to, and instructions in using a Soviet code. Subsequently, he bought a large, complex Hallicrafter short-wave receiver and installed it in his home, explaining to acquaintances that a friend of his, an American officer stationed in Paris who was a radio amateur, had got him interested in listening in on amateur short-wave broadcasts.

Wennerström spent four years working at the Command Office in Stockholm, and they were probably his most active years as an agent for Soviet Intelligence. During that time, the Swedish government, while it did not change its policy of neutrality, did make drastic changes in the nation's defenses. Stockholm is less than fifteen minutes by jet bomber from Soviet territory across the Baltic, and less than five minutes away by short-range missile. Since the mid-nineteen-fifties, the Swedish government has been pouring the equivalent of billions of dollars into an elaborate defense complex, including a system of secret airfields; huge underground submarine and destroyer pens blasted out of rock cliffs along the east coast; a radar network; an army of seven hundred thousand men; and the fourth or fifth most powerful air force in the world, using supersonic jet fighters and backed by ground-to-air non-nuclear missiles. Through the Command Office, Wennerström had access to secret documents concerning most of these developments.

At first, Wennerström testified, the information he passed on from Stockholm had primarily to do with American military planes and their electronic navigational equipment. Wennerström also reported, as he had been asked to do, on movements of American military personnel to Stockholm from the Pentagon and from United States Air Force headquarters in Wiesbaden. Then, in response to requests from the General, whom he continued periodically to meet in Helsinki, East Berlin, or the Soviet Union, he became more and more involved in obtaining information about American equipment used in the Swedish defense system. As head of the Air Section, he had the official task of keeping the Defense Ministry up to date on developments in guided missiles, and he was able to collect a great deal of highly detailed secret information on several Allied guided-missile systems, including the American air-to-air Sidewinder and ground-to-air Hawk. Also, he energetically continued to give the Russians detailed information, as he got it, on the American HM-55, which the Swedes were now using, and about which he had already reported in great detail from Washington.

In 1959, Wennerström met the General twice in Helsinki, and both times the General talked to him at length of growing Soviet fears that Sweden's air defenses were being secretly incorporated into the NATO system. Wennerström found his friend's exposition of the grounds for these fears so convincing that he began giving Soviet Intelligence increasing amounts of secret information on purely Swedish air-defense matters. He handed over documents concerning the design and operational characteristics of Sweden's highly advanced supersonic fighter, the Draken, and, eventually, a large mass of information on an elaborate computer-linked radar-warning and fire-control system known as Stril/ 60, the components of which were set up in deep rock emplacements throughout the country.

Because of Wennerström's extraordinarily ready access to secret documents, and because of his colleagues' trust in his discretion, he was able to take secret material home quite easily, and there, he later said, he did most of his surreptitious photographing of documents when the rest of his family was asleep. Wennerström's home was a large, well-furnished villa in Djursholm, a suburb that stands in relation to Stockholm approximately as Scarsdale does to New York. Wennerström had bought the house in 1957 for forty thousand dollars, paying a little less than half of that sum in cash. Although the Wennerströms drove a secondhand Rambler station wagon, which they had brought over from the United States—and which, Wennerström frequently told acquaintances, he had bought on the installment plan—and practiced certain other apparent economies, they lived, if not luxuriously, very comfortably. (After a while, Wennerström acquired a second car, a Saab station wagon, which, he said, he considered "an item of necessity" for his surreptitious business; he charged its cost and upkeep off to Soviet Intelligence.)

The Wennerströms entertained a great deal, seeing mostly members of the diplomatic set and, to a lesser extent, Swedish military people. The Wennerström's living standards were sufficiently high to cause their friends to doubt that the family was supported solely by the Colonel's military pay, but most of those who knew them assumed that their relative affluence was attributable to Mrs. Wennerström. Ulla Margareta Wennerström was a tall, good-looking woman thirteen years younger than her husband, with a gay and carefree manner. She was the daughter of Eric Valfrid Carlsson, a well-to-do former business manager of the newspaper *Stockholms-Tidningen,* and it seems that Carlsson in fact did give the Wennerströms some financial help from time to time. A few of Wennerström's acquaintances seem to have assumed, also, that his comfortable situation could be traced to some astute investments he had made while in the United States. Under these circumstances, there was no great reason for people to question the scale of the Wennerströms' living and entertaining—especially since it was known that in the case of the latter there were supplemental government entertainment allowances for diplomats.

As for whatever doubts Mrs. Wennerström might have developed about her husband's non-governmental activities or his sources of extra income, he later explained that he tried to forestall these by intimating that he was carrying on various investment transactions with one Dr. Gunther Prey, a wealthy businessman of Dutch citizenship who frequently came to Stockholm and with whom Wennerström professed a rather close friendship. There is, in fact, no evidence whatever that Wennerström actually had any financial dealings with Prey or that Prey was in any way aware of Wennerström's illegal activities. Mrs. Wennerström said after the Colonel's arrest that she had simply been content to leave family financial matters to her husband, whom she characterized as habitually "calm, secure, and clearheaded." Their financial situation was kept on an even keel, she believed, by her husband's budgeting, which she described as efficient to the point of being "almost stingy" at times.

Among his acquaintances in Djursholm, Wennerström seems to have been regarded as a pleasant and tactful host, a man of the world who, if he had no taste for profound or complicated political discussions, was in general pro-American and anti-Soviet. Mrs. Zinaida Sohlman, the Russian-born wife of Rolf Sohlman, who had been Swedish Ambassador to Moscow during Wennerström's service there, has recalled that one day when she attended a lunch at the Wennerström's villa, Wennerström drove her home. "I ventured the guess that the Russians in Stockholm were in as much an isolated situation as the Swedes in Moscow," she said. "Then Wennerström exploded. Never before had I seen such burning hatred as that which he displayed against the Russians. It was something so horrid as to make me almost shudder." Similarly, several colleagues of Wennerström's remember that once, during a meeting at the Command Office in 1959 at which arrangements for the impending visit of a Soviet military delegation were being discussed, Wennerström appeared considerably annoyed when someone remarked that the Soviet delegation ought to be provided with first-class plane tickets, saying sharply that economy passage should be quite good enough for such people. But such outspoken remarks were very unusual on his part. People who came in contact with him have indicated that they thought of him as having, beyond his supposed pro-Western inclinations, no particular deep convictions. And, for all his social graces, they found him guarded and aloof.

In his interrogation by the Swedish security police, Wennerström showed a certain pride in the efficiency and thoroughness with which, in his opinion, he had carried on not only his diplomatic work at the Defense Ministry but also his espionage activities for Soviet Intelligence. Of his transmission of microfilmed documents and books to his Soviet contacts, he remarked that "my ability to deliver was much greater than the receiver's capacity to work upon the material." Be-

tween the time Wennerström left Washington and the
time he was arrested, he transmitted to Soviet Intelligence a quantity of microfilm that has been estimated
to contain something between twenty thousand and
thirty thousand exposures, bearing perhaps as many
as five million words of text, along with innumerable
drawings and plans. The mass of words included Wennerström's espionage reports to the General, which he
typed out, usually in English but sometimes in German. (He was equally proficient in the two languages.)
According to Wennerström, he had begun writing these
reports to the General, at the General's suggestion,
while he was in Washington, and doing so had become
a regular habit. The letters reflected a close teamwork
between him and the General, and he used them to
"report so thoroughly that he [the General] got a complete insight into my whole life, and so it was of course
easier for him to give me suitable assignments and to
limit my assignments in a suitable way," Wennerström
testified, adding, "Later on, he had a quite clear
impression of all my acquaintances of various nation-
alities, so that he could at least guess whether I would
be able to carry out a certain assignment." He also
said, though, that the letters were not limited to reporting, however thorough, and explained their further
significance in this way:

Of course it is psychologically wearing to live a double
life for such a long time, where one life is the normal
existence and the other is a secret existence that you have
nobody to talk to about. I don't believe that this has such
a dangerous significance if you keep it up for a few
months or a year or perhaps two years. But when it begins
to be a long span of years, when it gets beyond ten years,
then it does become psychologically of powerful significance whether you [are able to] talk openly with any

other person. And I could do that with the General when
we met, but that was not often enough, and this correspondence became a surrogate. And it was not purely
business correspondence, where I talked about this or
that opportunity having opened up from the intelligence
point of view; I mixed in my personal experiences along
with these things — difficulties I had had or certain things
that one might be uneasy about, and later I mixed in pure
descriptions of affairs I had been present at and how
oddly things could work out. I took up purely family
circumstances and my interest in sports [Wennerström
was an enthusiast of the winter sport of curling] and every
possible thing of that sort.

At home at night, when Wennerström usually typed
out and photographed these letters to his old friend,
he carefully burned the originals in a cast-iron frying
pan that he kept in an open fireplace, and he flushed
the ashes down a toilet. Sometimes Wennerström typed
out reports to the General right in his office on Freds-
gatan, a street not far from the Foreign Office building,
and when doing so, if he found himself in doubt about
some technical detail, he would pick up the telephone,
place a call to someone in one of the Swedish ministries
who could clarify the problem, and then insert the
detail into his report. At his office, Wennerström had
another camera with which he could photograph espionage material, including letters to the General. When
he had finished photographing one of these letters at
his office, he would usually tear off all blank areas of
the paper and put them into a wastebasket. That left
only that part of the paper actually covered by writing
for him to destroy, and this he burned in an ashtray.
Then he mixed up the flakes of paper ash with a pencil
and emptied them into an envelope, which he took
home to dispose of. Later, at an appropriate time, he

would convey the exposed film to his local Russian
contact by one of several means, not dissimilar to those
he had used in Washington. Very occasionally, Wennerström's contact would relay to him personal notes
from the General. These were very brief and were
confined to birthday congratulations, New Year's
greetings, or thanks for materials that Wennerström
had sent. The written instructions he received from
the General were also brief; they were in Russian, and
seldom ran longer than half a page.

On his short-wave radio, Wennerström listened to
special coded broadcasts from the Soviet Union on a
regular basis. They consisted of a series of five-digit
numbers delivered by voice transmission. If they were
like broadcasts known to have been sent to other Soviet
agents, the messages probably were preceded in each
case by an identification signal of three spoken letters
repeated continuously for approximately two minutes.
Although the Swedish security police have been silent
on the subject, the Swedish press has published reports
that Wennerström was able to transmit radio messages
to the Soviet Union from his home. However that may
be, Wennerström seems to have continued to use his
local Soviet contact and what he called "the film route"
as his principal means of communicating with Moscow. Toward the end of Wennerström's service at the
Command Office, he increased his espionage activities
to the point where his local Soviet contact was hard
put to it to keep him from running out of unexposed
microfilm. Indeed, the prosecutor at Wennerström's
trial for treason in 1963 observed that "toward the end
his activities reached such a particularly hectic scope
that it is difficult to understand how he was able to
perform his legal work in line of duty."

In 1960, according to Wennerström, he was able to
accomplish what Moscow told him was "the best haul

I had made... since leaving the U.S.A." (The Swedes have not divulged any details, except the "haul" consisted of a secret document or documents.) He said that this "occasioned such an unusual reaction that the supreme chief of the [Military] Intelligence service in Moscow asked through my contact man in Moscow that it be arranged, if possible, for him to have a chance to meet me." During his next vacation, in September 1960, Wennerström managed to get himself and his wife invited to pay a private visit to the Swedish Embassy in Moscow, and while he was in Russia, he testified, he had three long meetings with Soviet Intelligence.

The first took place in Leningrad, where he was driven to an apartment on the northeastern edge of the city and there had a reunion with the General and handed over espionage material he had brought with him. The two succeeding meetings, he said, were held in Moscow. At the next, the General was waiting for him in a car at a pre-arranged point, and they were driven to a house that Wennerström recognized as one of his meeting places with the General in the old days when he was Sweden's air attaché in Moscow. After being given instructions for future espionage work, he was told that the head of Soviet Military Intelligence wanted to see him the following day. Late the next morning, he was taken to an apartment, where he met the General and exchanged his Western-style overcoat for a Russian one, and then the two men were driven to a house, where, he said, a Soviet four-star general (whose name Wennerström apparently did not learn) was waiting for them. They were served caviar sandwiches and vodka, he said, and the four-star general made a speech praising Wennerström's achievements—in particular, Wennerström's "best haul," which, the four-star general said, was so useful that it had saved Russia several years of research and a great deal of expense. Wennerström said that the Soviet Military Intelligence chief then told him that by virtue of his long and effective service on behalf of Soviet Intelligence he had earned three Soviet decorations, which the four-star general had with him. Pointing out that it would, of course, be too dangerous for Wennerström to take the medals back to Sweden, the four-star general handed the three medals over to Wennerström's co-worker for safekeeping, and, according to Wennerström, "further said that I was entitled to draw a salary from Russian Intelligence as long as I lived. . . ."

Directly after the visit to Moscow, Wennerström and his wife went to Spain for a short while. He said later that he had been requested by Soviet Intelligence to reestablish contact there with American officers whom he had known in the United States. His retirement from active service as a Swedish Air Force officer was now only about a year off, and, according to his testimony, for some time prior to the Moscow visit the General had indicated that the Soviet Intelligence service wanted him to move to Spain after his retirement and continue his espionage activities there—reporting, in particular, on American air bases on Spanish soil and American naval operations in the Mediterranean. The General, it seemed, had also told Wennerström that to prepare for the Spanish assignment he would need to enroll at some time in a special course in geodesy that was given in the Soviet Union, and Wennerström testified that he concluded from this that his activities in Spain would include the pinpointing of American nuclear-missile bases as targets for Soviet missiles. Geodesy is the science of determining the exact position of points on the earth's surface, and preparations for the use of missiles require that the relative positions of target and firing site on the earth's surface be measured with immense precision.

At about this time, there was talk that Sweden and Spain might exchange military attachés—something that they had never previously done—and Wennerström said later that he had thought briefly of seeking the post of Swedish air attaché in Madrid, which would, of course, have given him the ideal vantage point for continuing his activities for Soviet Intelligence. Soon, however, the Swedes cooled toward the attaché notion, and in any event, Wennerström said, he began having second thoughts about taking his children away from Sweden again, so as the time for his retirement grew closer he cast about for another job in Sweden. He has indicated that there was some talk of his going into a business owned by one of his wife's relatives, and that he had a couple of other commercial offers. He also applied for a civilian post that was open on the Swedish Air Force staff—the post of duty officer, which may have been particularly interesting to Wennerström because it involved the handling of all incoming and outgoing documents, classified and unclassified. Wennerström was favored for the job, but before the position was filled he was called into the office of the Swedish Defense Minister, Sven Andersson, who told him that the Foreign Minister, Östen Undén, was looking for an experienced officer to serve as military adviser to the Foreign Office on disarmament problems. Wennerström thought about this overnight, and, he said later, concluded that although his access to secret documents would be somewhat reduced, from an espionage point of view "it was ever so much better to be sitting in the Foreign Office than with the Air Force Staff," because "you get a much broader view from there." Besides, he said, making a characteristic point, "I was aware that as far as my

personal prestige vis-à-vis the Soviet Intelligence service was concerned, it would rise considerably from
my getting into the Foreign Office." Formally, at least,
he would be working under the direct orders of the
Foreign Minister.

Wennerström accepted the job and sent off a letter
to the General telling him, he has said, that he thought
the arrangement "extraordinarily good." He transferred
to the Foreign Office in October of 1961, and in No-
vember he made still another trip to Helsinki for a
secret meeting with the General, who, according to
Wennerström, reiterated his interest in information
bearing on possible changes in Sweden's neutrality.
Wennerström told him that Sweden was preparing to
make a broad survey to determine whether the country's defense system should be reorganized, and the
General asked him to find out whether such a reorgani-
zation might be aimed at making it possible for American forces to land in Sweden. The General also told
Wennerström that the Soviet government was very
uneasy about the American development of the Polaris
submarine and, in particular, about the possibility that
such submarines might be able to enter the Baltic. He
said that in case they did, his government had to consider means of intervening against them, and that the
means included not only counter-measures by the Soviet Navy but bombing by Soviet planes equipped with
nuclear weapons. Here, he said, Swedish anti-aircraft
defenses were an important consideration, because it
would be necessary for the Soviet anti-submarine
bombers to fly over Sweden.

At the end of the meeting, the General told Wennerström that he would be provided with a new contact
man in Stockholm. The General and Wennerström then
agreed that they would meet next in Vienna, in June
1962. However, according to Wennerström, this meet-

ing was later canceled through a radio message from the Soviet Union, and he subsequently learned not only that the cancelation was connected with the Soviet preparations leading to the Cuban missile crisis but that the General was in Cuba himself, directing Soviet Intelligence activities there.

Wennerström has said that, as for his own part in the Cuban affair, to help the Soviets avoid miscalculation during the crisis he made a report, based on talks that he had with American diplomats and military and naval officers in Stockholm at the time, to the Soviet Intelligence service on American intentions. And he has said that as a result, his local Soviet contact relayed a message to him about a month after the Cuban crisis conveying "special thanks" from the four-star general, by whom he had been decorated in Moscow, for the information.

At the Foreign Office, Wennerström became technical adviser on disarmament to the Foreign Minister and to the Swedish disarmament commission, whose chairman was Alva Myrdal, the wife of the famous sociologist Gunnar Myrdal. The commission participated in the 1961 disarmament negotiations in Geneva, and Wennerström testified that his position made it possible for him to give an extra push to courses of action favored by the Soviets. Wennerström's colleagues on the commission seem to have been entirely unsuspicious of his motives. "I found him to be very knowledgeable. He seemed to be *in* on so many things," one of these people has said. "We took him for a true expert on military matters. He seemed more interested in disarmament than is common among military people. His manner was kind, amiable, and very self-assured. He never gesticulated, never showed surprise; his face was almost serene. He was very discreet.

When we had a meeting with the Foreign Minister, he would never speak first, but when someone called upon him to give the facts about something he would answer with a gleam in his eye. He seemed proud to know things that others didn't."

Five

ONE THING THAT WENNERSTRÖM'S CO-WORKERS ON the disarmament commission did not know and that he did not know, either, was that his own activities had for some time been a matter of interest to the Swedish security police. Indeed, the security people had had intimations as far back as the Second World War that Wennerström was not the best possible risk, but nothing much had been done at the time. In 1941, after Wennerström, then a captain, had returned from his first tour of duty as Swedish air attaché in Moscow, the security people noticed that he had unusually close associations with both Russian and German diplomats in Stockholm—especially the latter—but they certainly did not realize that while Wennerström was in Moscow he had been supplying the Nazis with information on Soviet military matters. Early in 1943, the Swedes succeeded in breaking the code used by the German Embassy in Stockholm, and they found, in a cable to Berlin from the German military attaché, the name of Wennerström, who was cited as a source of information about the Soviet Union. In order not to tip the Germans off to the fact that the code had been broken, the Swedish security people refrained from calling Wennerström in for questioning, but they did tap his telephone and place his mail under surveillance. However, these measures yielded no further evidence that he was engaged in illegal intelligence activities, and the use of his name by the Germans was ascribed to an indiscretion on his part rather than to any willful act, so the surveillance was dropped.

In 1947 and 1948, when Wennerström was with the Swedish Air Force Staff, he again became the subject of attention by the security police when he was reported to be in "lively" contact with Soviet air attaché Rybachenko. But when the security people discussed the matter with Gustaf Adolf Westring, chief of the Swedish Air Force Staff, who was then a colonel, Westring, it is said, shrugged their suspicions off as "mere gossip." Again, nothing was done. No further suspicion seems to have attached to Wennerström until 1958 or so, when an inspector in the Swedish security police, Otto Danielsson, happened to come across an official report that Wennerström had written in 1947. It was a report on the "legal," or overt, intelligence activities of the Soviet military attaché in Stockholm, and Danielsson has said that he found it striking because it showed "a little too much insight" into the workings of the Soviet Military Intelligence apparatus. But when Danielsson discussed the matter with several military-intelligence men, they found it perfectly plausible that Wennerström, with his knowledge of Soviet affairs and of Soviet diplomatic personnel, could have been able to get close enough to the Soviet military attaché to describe his work in some detail. No move was made against Wennerström on the basis of his 1947 report. (And, indeed, it would have been somewhat ironic had any move been made on that basis, since, according to all the evidence, Wennerström was not in fact recruited by the Russians until the end of 1948.)

In 1959, while returning by commercial airplane from Britain, where he had attended a Royal Air Force flying show at Farnborough, Wennerström left the airplane during a stopover at Amsterdam under circumstances that one of his fellow Swedish delegates found suspicious. This fact was reported to the Swedish security people, and Wennerström's office at the Command Office was searched. The search yielded nothing except a handbook on photography, but because Danielsson was by now more suspicious of Wennerström, a tap was again placed on his telephone, by secret court order.

The tapping didn't yield much information, and after a year or so the security police had trouble justifying its continuance. In Sweden, where the rights of individuals are jealously protected by the courts—jealously protected, even, by court prosecutors—a good prima-facie case has to be made before a court will order wire-tapping, and after such an order is given, monthly judicial hearings have to be held to renew it. (As for illegal wire-tapping by security agencies in Sweden, it appears to be unheard of.) In 1960, the Defense Minister, Sven Andersson, was told of the suspicions about Wennerström, but, in the absence of concrete evidence, no move was made to restrict his access to secret documents. In September 1961, when the wire-tapping was about to be stopped, Wennerström's car was seen one day parked near a place where police had reason to believe that Soviet agents had maintained a dead drop, so the surveillance was continued.

Wennerström's application for the job of duty officer on the Air Force Staff was so disturbing to the security people that the Defense Minister was asked to prevent him from accepting it, and it was for this reason that the Minister offered him the disarmament job. "There, thank God, he will be harmless," Andersson is said to have told Georg Thulin, the head of the Swedish security police. But it may be that there is no such thing as a harmless position for a spy— certainly not a position in which the spy happens to be known to his unsuspecting colleagues under the high-sounding title of Military Adviser to the Foreign Minister. For fear Wennerström would be warned that he was under surveillance, the security police told only one or two of his superiors what was afoot. Behind all this caution there seems to have been not only a laudable apprehension about violating Wennerström's rights but also a vast reluctance to believe that a senior Swedish officer who was a member of a respectable military family and a veteran diplomat could be engaged in espionage activities.

At a security briefing in March 1962, the Defense Minister was given a review of the suspicions against Wennerström. The extent of his association with the Soviet air attaché was discussed, and so was a claim Wennerström had made to a colleague that he was under orders from Foreign Minister Östen Undén to cultivate Soviet personnel for the purpose of obtaining information on the Soviet attitude toward disarmament questions. The Foreign Minister said that he hadn't told Wennerström anything of the sort, but added that he could see how Wennerström could legitimately have come to feel that he *was* under such orders. The Defense Minister and the head of the security police are reported to have agreed that while certain things looked suspicious, "Wennerström, despite it all, could be innocent, and . . . in its entirety what had been cited against him could have a natural explanation," in the words of a subsequent Swedish security report. On this occasion, the Minister of Justice, according to the same report, "expressed some surprise" that the court had permitted Wennerström's telephone to be tapped, but, perhaps because he "wanted to unshoulder part of the burden of what he had been told," the Minister of Justice also said that he thought the Prime Minister, Tage Erlander, should be briefed on the Wennerström case. Accordingly, a date was set for the Prime Minister to be informed about what was described to him as "a matter concerning a colonel in the Foreign Office against whom vague suspicions had been directed that he might be a security risk." But then the prosecutor who was supposed to make the briefing got sick, and the briefing was postponed. As it happened, the Prime Minister was too busy to attend the next scheduled briefing on Wennerström, and after that the Minister of Justice was out of the country for a time, and the upshot was that the whole thing somehow slid off the Prime Minister's calendar. Nobody seemed to have the stomach for it.

In September 1962, Torsten Nilsson took over as Foreign Minister, and though he was informed of certain suspicions against Wennerström at that time, it was not until early December that the pressure of work allowed a complete briefing on the case. He declared that there seemed to be "hardly anything concrete that one could put one's finger on," and said he was surprised that in Sweden "on such vague grounds a person could be exposed to wire-tapping." At another briefing, on December 6, there was talk of easing Wennerström out of his job at the Foreign Office, but the

Foreign Minister protested that "if [Wennerström] should be innocent, a dismissal would imply a violation of his integrity," and that if he should be guilty, he would at once realize that he was under suspicion, and would be harder to uncover. In June 1962, the Defense Minister had issued a carefully worded general order that was meant to have the effect of restricting Wennerström's access to classified documents. It went to the Foreign Office and the Defense Command but, for some bureaucratic reason, didn't reach an obscure department called the Defense Books and Forms Warehouse, which, as it happened, was perhaps Wennerström's most important source of Swedish secret information, since he could draw classified material from it at will.

The persistent Inspector Danielsson had not given up his suspicions, and the wire-tapping went on. And on December 11, 1962, the security police, listening in on a telephone conversation between Wennerström's younger daughter and a friend, heard her remark that her father had "the world's strangest radio," to which she couldn't listen, because her father had to "pick up Russia or whatever it is." She added that if she went near the radio her father cried "No!" At that point, police surveillance of Wennerström was intensified. On January 10, 1963, the police noted that the First Secretary of the Soviet Embassy in Stockholm, Georgi Baranovsky, telephoned Wennerström to say that "a special book on the disarmament question" had been mailed to him from Moscow. The police found the conversation somewhat labored. (Actually, it concerned the transmission of espionage instructions from the General.) For all that, few of the responsible Swedes concerned could bring themselves to contemplate seriously the idea that Wennerström was a spy. Early in May 1963, the head of the Swedish security police told a colleague that "in spite of everything, I believe deep down inside that he is innocent." By that time, the police had found out that Wennerström had been borrowing all sorts of secret documents from the Defense Books and Forms Warehouse, and that he was also trying to obtain information from other sources about Swedish defenses.

The security people, still feeling that they didn't have sufficient grounds for an arrest, briefly considered questioning a woman named Mrs. Carin Rosén, who worked as a part-time maid at Wennerström's house, about his activities, but, out of continued caution, they hesitated to approach Mrs. Rosén. Interestingly enough, while the security people were wondering whether to get in touch with Mrs. Rosén, it happened that she was wondering whether to get in touch with them. Mrs. Rosén, the wife of a retired noncommissioned naval officer, seems to have been exceptionally alert. She had gone to work for the Wennerströms in October 1957, not long after they returned from Washington, coming to the villa at Djursholm just one day a week. Later, she came twice a week, and, still later, three times. The house had ten rooms, but for some time Mrs. Rosén had had to clean only nine of them; she found that the door of the tenth room—which was on the ground floor, next to a room that Wennerström used as a study—was usually locked. Mrs. Rosén later said that when she arrived in the morning, at seven-thirty, Wennerström was always up, wearing a bathrobe, and that he seemed to spend considerable time in the locked room before he shaved and dressed.

In the spring of 1958, Wennerström moved his study up to the second floor of the house, and thereafter the mysterious ground-floor room was kept locked only when he was busy in it. From time to time, when he wasn't home, Mrs. Rosén would go in to clean it up.

It seemed to her to be some sort of rubbish room, containing old clothing, folding card tables, and so on. At one end, a curtain hung from ceiling to floor, and on pushing the curtain to one side Mrs. Rosén saw behind it a file cabinet, a safe with a combination lock, and, under a dust cover, some sort of photographic apparatus. At the base of the apparatus were a couple of lamps on flexible mounts. Mrs. Rosén assumed that Wennerström must be an amateur photographer, and that his hobby must be what occupied him early in the morning, and she thought no more of the matter for quite a while. Eventually, though, she became mildly puzzled at never seeing any photographs around the house.

Mrs. Rosén found the Wennerströms "a nice family" and Wennerström himself pleasant and considerate. She noticed that he seemed to read quite a bit, and among the books she saw him reading were *Modern Russian Humor* and spy stories called *Behind the Iron Curtain, The Gauntlet Is Thrown,* and *Nights in Prague*. She decided that Wennerström must have quite a bit of money of his own. Because she had worked for Swedish military people before, she knew that a colonel's base pay was about thirty thousand kronor, and while the Wennerströms didn't live extravagantly they lived above that level. They gave a good many luncheon and dinner parties, at which she assisted. One of the daytime parties was for the Wennerströms' younger daughter, and Mrs. Rosén said that in connection with the affair she suggested casually to Mrs. Wennerström that somebody ought to take a picture of the girl. Mrs. Rosén has said that to her surprise Mrs. Wennerström told her that there was nobody in the family who could take a decent photograph.

This made Mrs. Rosén think that something was very odd—especially since she had seen rolls of film tucked away near the photographic apparatus—but after a while it occurred to her that perhaps Wennerström was doing some sort of photographic copying in connection with his official work. She also worked part time for a man who was employed on the Defense Staff, and she asked him one day whether he often had work to do after office hours. When he said he sometimes did, she asked him whether he ever had to bring papers home to photograph. He seemed astonished at the question, and answered that of course he never did that. However, he wasn't astonished enough to ask Mrs. Rosén why she wanted to know, and she didn't enlighten him.

Her own perplexity grew. It occurred to her next that if Wennerström wasn't doing his photography in connection with his official work, he might be doing it in connection with some other kind of work, to make extra money. Then, one day when the Wennerströms were giving a dinner party, Wennerström went with Mrs. Rosén to get a pair of silver trays out of the safe in the rubbish room. Upon bending down next to the safe to take the trays from him, she saw several "thick stacks of money" tied together by paper bands. The bills looked new. At that moment, there occurred to Mrs. Rosén another possible explanation for Wennerström's photographic activity—that he was in the pornography business. Then an even more shocking thought came to her—that he was counterfeiting Swedish currency. Mrs. Rosén was used to being paid by the Wennerströms in new ten-kronor bills, and now, on the pretext that the fresh bills tended to stick together, she asked to be paid in used bills. The request was granted so easily that she felt obliged to dismiss the counterfeiting theory.

There finally came to Mrs. Rosén the notion that Wennerström's clandestine work was somehow con-

nected with "the spy war between Russia and America." One day in the spring of 1960, when Wennerström
was busy in the "rubbish room," the telephone rang.
Mrs. Rosén answered it, and called out to Wennerström that someone from the Defense Staff was on the
line. Wennerström emerged, leaving the door slightly
ajar, and while he was taking the call, Mrs. Rosén
peeked into the "rubbish room." Near the photographic
apparatus stood a card table, and on it were some sheets
of black paper with white outlines on them, which
looked like technical drawings of some kind. Mrs.
Rosén now began to consider seriously whether Wennerström might be a spy for a foreign power and whether
his photographic work might be directed against Sweden. Shortly afterward, she began noticing evidence
of paper having been burned from time to time in the
frying pan in the fireplace. She was at a loss as to
where to turn with this strange information. She didn't
want to tell her husband, because she was afraid he
might think she was out of her mind, and she didn't
feel that the "regular" police were the people to go to
with such a story. She looked in the telephone book
to see if "Spy Police" or "Security Police" appeared
there, but she found no such listings. (Actually, the
Swedish name for the security police was "Statspoli-
sen"—"State Police.") Having made this effort, Mrs.
Rosén took no further action. Her suspicions, however, remained.

In the fall of 1960, Wennerström went abroad for
more than a month, and on his return he gave Mrs.
Rosén a small bottle of perfume, which he said he had
bought for her in Paris. When Mrs. Rosén showed the
bottle to her daughter, her daughter noticed a tiny label
bearing the letters "NK" on it. In Stockholm, "NK"
is known as the initials of Nordiska Kompaniet, the
biggest department store in the city, so Mrs. Rosén

suspected that Wennerström's story about having been to Paris was false. (Wennerström's journeys in the fall of 1960 had taken him to Leningrad and Moscow and then to Spain. He probably did stop off in Paris on his way back to Stockholm from Madrid, so it is likely that the perfume that aroused Mrs. Rosén's suspicions represented simply an attempt to correct an oversight, Wennerström perhaps having bought the bottle at the last minute in Stockholm when he belatedly realized that the maid might be disappointed if she received no present from Paris.)

From this point on, Mrs. Rosén seems to have thrown herself into amateur detective work with a will. She noticed, after one of Wennerström's trips abroad, that he had installed a new and very complicated-looking radio set in his study. Near it on a wall was a loud-speaker, from which, however, she never heard a sound. The set was equipped with a pair of earphones, and Mrs. Rosén decided to check up on the extent to which Wennerström used his curious radio, so when she did her cleaning in the study, she occasionally placed tiny flakes of paint on top of the earphones and then looked to see how often they were disturbed; on the basis of these indications she concluded that Wennerström listened to the radio on certain fixed days of the week. She made similar efforts to find out how much Wennerström was using his photographic apparatus, taking tiny pieces of down from a bird cage and putting them in the eyes of a pair of scissors that were kept near the apparatus.

Mrs. Rosén also noticed, in the best Holmes tradition, the curious behavior of two dogs who were a part of the Wennerström household. One day in 1961, she said, she met, on a stairway of the Wennerström house, a man she described as "the Russian"; from newspaper pictures she discovered him to be Major

General Vitaly Nikolsky, then military attaché at the Soviet Embassy. Mrs. Rosén noticed that "the Russian" seemed to be quite at home in the Wennerström household—so much so that the two Wennerström dogs, who invariably barked at strangers, failed to react to his presence at all.

In the spring of 1963, Mrs. Rosén felt that she had new grounds for suspicion. On April 10, the Wennerströms gave a cocktail party, and in preparation for it Mrs. Rosén was asked to tidy up the rubbish room so that it could be used as a cloakroom. In doing so, she happened to notice a brown paper bag tucked between the safe and the wall. Looking inside the bag, she found that it contained several wrapped rolls of film. She removed three of these, took them into a nearby room, closed the door, and opened the packages. She could see nothing on the film, and, with some difficulty, she put it back in the containers. She put the rolls back where she had found them, and at the end of the party she noticed that the brown paper bag was gone.

Mrs. Rosén still couldn't bring herself to go to the police with the story of what she had observed. A year or so earlier, she had thought that she might make a telephone call to Torsten Nilsson, then the Minister of Social Welfare, both because she felt, from what she had heard about him, that he was "a man one could talk to" and because they both "belonged to the same political party"—the Social Democrats. But while she was still considering the idea, Nilsson became Foreign Minister, and after that she didn't dare call him, because he was such an important man. Thus, Nilsson, the Minister for whom Wennerström worked, just missed getting some concrete evidence from the one person who could really have helped with the case.

On May 16, 1963, however, two men from the

Swedish security police decided to call on Mrs. Rosén at her home. First, they told her how difficult it was, in the light of Swedish law and the principles of democratic justice, for the police to accuse someone suspected of a crime against Sweden without having firm evidence. Then one of the men told Mrs. Rosén that the suspect they had come to ask her about was Colonel Wennerström. Observing Mrs. Rosén's reaction, the agent told her that she didn't seem very much surprised. She replied that she wasn't.

On June 19, Mrs. Rosén, at work in the Wennerströms' attic, noticed that a flower urn she had set down in a bin full of sawdust some days before was resting at a different angle. She rummaged around in the sawdust and found several packets, wrapped in gray paper and sealed with tape, that she felt sure contained film. She quietly went to the telephone and notified the security police. Then, following their instructions, she put two of the packets in her handbag.

The following morning, Wennerström, on his way to work, parked his car near a government building and started to walk across a bridge called the Riksbron toward the Foreign Office. As he did so, two black cars pulled up and blocked both ends of the bridge. A security-police officer got out of one, approached Wennerström, introduced himself, shook hands, and informed Wennerström that he was under arrest on suspicion of espionage. Wennerström reacted with perfect outward calm.

At the headquarters of the security police, Wennerström at first firmly denied any wrongdoing. The police, however, soon were able to confront him with impressive evidence, much of which they obtained through searches of his house, in support of their charge. It included written instructions from the Soviet Intel-

ligence service concerning future espionage tasks, and
a few charred fragments of military documents that
Wennerström had burned in his fireplace at home after
making photographic copies of them, but which Mrs.
Rosén had been able to retrieve and hand over to the
authorities. Also, in Wennerström's house, the police
found a bundle of Swedish banknotes totaling fifteen
thousand kronor, or three thousand dollars. Upon being
shown all these items, Wennerström declared that they
had to do with work that he had been performing as
an agent for a movement to undermine the Soviet re-
gime. Confronted with more evidence, he conceded
that he had indeed spied for the Soviet Union—but,
he maintained, only against the United States, not
against Sweden. Then, however, the security police
came up with still more damning evidence, which they
had possibly acquired by discovering a way to develop
Wennerström's special film.

Wennerström thought things over, and, on the third
day after his arrest, announced that he wanted to tell
the truth. He admitted that he had been a Soviet agent
for fifteen years and that he had in fact spied against
Sweden, and he said that when he was arrested he had
been about to flee the country. He explained that the
evening before his arrest he had discovered the loss
of the two packets of film—and had realized that his
situation was very dangerous. Later that evening, he
had gone with his wife to a diplomatic party at the
United States Embassy, stopping off briefly at his office on the way to the party to make sure that, through
some mixup, he hadn't left the film there. From the
Embassy, he had slipped away for an emergency meeting with his current Soviet contact man, Major General
Nikolsky, who had given him the fifteen thousand
kronor. At the time of his arrest, he said, he had been
planning an immediate departure by air for Spain, and

he had hoped subsequently to go to Vienna to attend a scheduled meeting with the General, with whom he had hoped to agree on a lump-sum payment of the hundreds of thousands of kronor he had estimated to have accrued to his account in Moscow for all of his previous services to the Russians.

Later, during his pre-trial interrogation, Wennerström said that while he regretted carrying on his espionage against Sweden itself, and had only done so under considerable pressure from the Russians, he had felt that his own national loyalty had to be subordinated to the solution of "larger international questions" (meaning, essentially, a balance of power between Russia and the United States, and hence world peace), and that he felt he had been working toward such a solution. He said that his predicament distressed him not for his own sake but for the sake of his family. Mrs. Wennerström's situation was, for a time after the arrest, a difficult one. She was intensively questioned by the Swedish security police, and although she swore that she knew nothing of her husband's espionage, the police informed her that she was under suspicion of complicity in Wennerström's activities. Whatever may be the answer to the riddle posed by the fact that Mrs. Rosén found Wennerström's films and elaborate photographic equipment and Mrs. Wennerström said she did not, it does seem reasonable to assume that Mrs. Wennerström, as the wife of a military man and a diplomat who regularly handled official secret documents, would, through the years, have developed a loyal habit of not expressing curiosity about such aspects of her husband's professional life. In any case, Swedish security police have never preferred any charges against Mrs. Wennerström.

Although Wennerström expressed concern for his family, he told his interrogators at the same time that

his own situation, although frightening, did not crush
him. He added that he felt this way either because he
was a fatalist or because he had achieved "extreme
nerve control" during his years of illegal intelligence
work, in which, he said, he had "faced many a ghastly
situation" requiring steady nerves and great self-dis-
cipline—a self-dramatizing description that suggests
some of the difficulties encountered by those who have
tried to distinguish the accuracies from the inaccuracies
in the long and painstakingly detailed account of his
activities that Wennerström gave his interrogators.

The news of Wennerström's arrest, his confession
that he had been a paid Soviet spy for so many years,
and reports of the extent to which he had betrayed
Swedish defense secrets sent a great wave of shock
through Sweden. The Supreme Commander of the
Swedish armed forces, General Torsten Rapp, probably summed up the national response when, addressing the nation on television, he said, "To me it is
unbelievable that a Swedish officer could lend himself
to anything of the sort. The occurrence quite naturally
has aroused deep gloom throughout the entire military
establishment." And the Stockholm daily *Expressen*,
whose circulation is the largest in Scandinavia, ran an
article declaring, "The Wennerström spying has
knocked out essential parts of Swedish defense
...Frantic measures are being taken to repair
any of the damage that can be repaired." There were
demands from all sides that the government explain
why Wennerström's spying had gone undetected for
so long, and in order to comply the government appointed a special commission of three judges to in-
vestigate the Wennerström affair. The commission's
report—made public in 1964—concluded that, taking
into account the full respect that must be maintained
for the constitutional rights of any Swedish citizen

under suspicion, it was essentially to Wennerström's "great skill and cunning" as an agent, rather than laxity on the part of the government security people, that his remarkably long career in espionage could be attributed.

Wennerström's arraignment was eventually set for October 26, 1963, but on the 24th he was rushed unconscious to a Stockholm hospital, having attempted suicide by taking a large number of sleeping pills. Because he had been complaining of headaches and sleeplessness, Wennerström, for some time previously, had been given sleeping pills under the eyes of guards who were constantly in his cell with him, but in spite of this supervision he had managed to hide a large stock of the barbiturates. The most striking thing about this episode is not Wennerström's ability to make his guards believe he was taking the pills when he was secretly accumulating them but, rather, the manner in which he managed to acquire them in the first place. Instead of telling his guards that he had to have sleeping pills every night, he asked for them only irregularly, saying that he didn't want to become dependent on them. It was this little aside that, as much as anything, disarmed the authorities.

The doctors at the hospital were able to pull Wennerström around fairly quickly, and after they had done so he was transferred to a psychiatric clinic at Långholmen Prison for examination. He was found to be sane and fully able to stand trial, and, after a second extended period of interrogation, he was finally arraigned in Stockholm in February 1964. His trial, by three judges in a Stockholm magistrate's court, was secret, and only brief summations by his lawyer and by the prosecutor, Werner Ryhninger, a final plea to the court by Wennerström, and part of the text of the judgment have been made public. (For security reasons, the remaining records of the trial were ordered sealed for fifty years.) The prosecutor declared in his published summation that "Wennerström's treason is the most serious one inflicted on our country in history." He described the accused as a vain opportunist who "with utter ruthlessness" had "exploited his official position and the confidence of his colleagues" for very considerable financial gain. And he demanded that Wennerström be given the maximum sentence under Swedish law, which is life imprisonment.

On behalf of Wennerström—whose attitude during the trial was described by someone present as "very cooperative" and whose bearing was called, by another person present, "calm and correct"—Carl-Elik Lindahl, a lawyer appointed for him by the court, declared that the motives behind his client's espionage were not financial but ideological: that it was "his ambition to serve the peace" that "separated Wennerström from his national ties." Wennerström told the court in his final plea, "My activities have been interwoven in the international Great Power espionage struggle which is a factor in the Cold War," and "During the years, I have gone through a gradual shift in outlook. At first, I was wholly devoted to working for NATO, and thereafter to working as an agent for both sides, until I finally decided to work exclusively for the Soviet Union. . . . Sweden was not the primary objective. I was working against a wider perspective. . . . I believe that the Soviet Union's course of peace and coexistence is seriously meant." He concluded his plea by saying, "I am fully prepared to stand the juridical consequences of my actions."

On June 12, the court found Wennerström guilty of gross espionage and sentenced him to life imprisonment at hard labor. The court also ruled that, since in his fifteen years of spying Wennerström had received from the Soviet Intelligence service approximately a hundred thousand dollars, exclusive of sums presumably still being held for him in Moscow, he was to be fined an amount equivalent to what he had actually received. In this matter, the court took note of Wennerström's objection to the prosecution's contention that the money he had not yet received from the Russians should also be subject to Swedish forfeiture. The court further ordered that Wennerström be stripped of his rank. Wennerström was informed of the judgment and the sentence in his cell at Långholmen Prison, and he was reported to have taken the news "with composure."

In the meantime, the affair had precipitated a national political crisis, in which the Social Democratic government of Tage Erlander barely avoided a parliamentary motion of censure. A month before this row, the government had approved the first installment of a special appropriation for the repair of the military damage caused Sweden by Wennerström's espionage. It was estimated that repairs, made over a period of seven years, would cost sixty million dollars. The damage to the morale of the Swedish military was perhaps even more costly. "I've seen tears come to the eyes of Swedish officers at the mention of the Wennerström case," a man attached to the United States Embassy in Stockholm said a while ago.

Six

THE NOTION THAT A RESPECTED SENIOR SWEDISH OF-
ficer should for years have been a double-dealer in
important military information with the great powers
and then have become a top Soviet agent holding the
rank of major general in the Soviet Intelligence service
has proved disturbing not only to the Swedes but to
people throughout the Western world who have read
accounts of the "Swedish master spy" and his activities. Yet Wennerström's story of his espionage work,
widely accepted though it may be, deserves further
examination, if only because a good deal of it is based
only on his version of events, and many of these events,
having occurred behind the Iron Curtain, are difficult
to check up on. It also deserves careful scrutiny in the
light of Wennerström's own personality, in the light
of his rather complex relations with his principal Soviet
contact, the General, and in the light of modern international espionage practices.

As I discovered when I went to Stockholm, the transcripts of Wennerström's pre-trial interrogations constitute the single most valuable source of information on the affair. Even though these had been censored heavily in places, by careful reading it was possible for me to fill in certain minor gaps, because the censorship, which had been done under great pressure, was not altogether uniform throughout the great mass of documents that the Swedish government had been obliged by political circumstances to make public.

When I arrived in Sweden, I had very little reason to doubt the extent and character of Wennerström's international espionage as contained in his confessions. However, after a lengthy talk with a high security official in a very well-protected office, I began to have doubts about the completeness of Wennerström's account of many events. As a result, I went back to the transcripts and read through them again and again, not simply as an outside observer but insofar as I could as though I myself might be a participant in the Wennerström affair. First I read them as I imagined things to be from Wennerström's point of view. Then I read the same transcripts again from what I thought might be the General's point of view, and so on, from one to another—the Americans with whom Wennerström dealt in Moscow, the people in Washington, the Swedish security people themselves. Gradually, in doing this, I came to realize that another and more complex story surely must underlie the long confession that Wennerström made in his pre-trial interrogation. With this in mind, I then approached a number of knowledgeable people in Stockholm and Washington with a great number of questions about the Soviet Intelligence system. The answers and comments I obtained pretty well confirmed my own analysis of what must really have happened in the Wenn-erström affair.

Perhaps a good starting point in an appraisal of Wennerström's story is his testimony on how he first became involved in United States Intelligence activi-ties against the Soviet Union by being persuaded by an American agent in Stockholm to mail a parcel con-taining radio tubes or similar equipment in Leningrad in 1946. It would be ironic if American Intelligence, rather than Soviet Intelligence, should prove to have been responsible for getting Wennerström started on his postwar career of international espionage. Shortly after his arrest, the United States Embassy in Stock-holm issued a statement to the effect that no record existed of his having been given any intelligence task by any American organization. In such cases, such statements naturally do not mean much, being in the nature of routine disclaimers. The Americans undoubt-edly had some secret agents operating in the Soviet Union in 1946, and the American organization most likely to know about the activities of these agents and what part, if any, Wennerström played in them is the Central Intelligence Agency—for, although it was not formed until 1947, it then took over the records and functions of the cloak-and-dagger Office of Strategic Services. Not surprisingly, the C.I.A. people have nothing to say about Wennerström, about his activities, or, for that matter, about the activities of the C.I.A. It happens, however, that the Agency—as the C.I.A. is known to many people in the Pentagon—is by no means the only American governmental organization engaged in what the participants, when they can be brought to discuss it at all, tend to refer to simply as "this business." There are in Washington at least six other substantial organizations—several of them with headquarters in the Pentagon—that have available to them a considerable body of information on the Wennerström affair. Of these specialized outfits, one, in particular, has made a very wide-ranging investigation of the Wennerström case, and a few results of this investigation, including Wennerström's account of his alleged contact with United States Intelligence in 1946, have recently been discussed, on the record, by certain people connected with it.

According to one of these men, even the most extensive search of government files and the most extensive interrogation of Intelligence people have failed to uncover any evidence that Wennerström did in fact carry out the 1946 mission he says he carried out. "The trouble is that we are, of course, unable to prove that Wennerström *wasn't* approached by an American agent in Stockholm in 1946," this Pentagon man said. "Wennerström says that an agent came to Stockholm from West Germany, and he could be correct in this. The fact that there is no record of such an approach in any Intelligence file we can get our hands on could be explained by the passage of time. You have to understand that in 1946 in Berlin there were between forty and fifty *known* United States Intelligence agencies, and they engaged in intensive competition. They didn't have a central body coördinating all this work, and the agents often tried to outfox one another, like a bunch of newspaper correspondents. The situation was pretty chaotic. It is quite possible that one of these organizations worked in Sweden. Most of them have long since become defunct, the personnel have gone their ways, and the records may have been destroyed as well."

As to Wennerström's having told his interrogators that the Americans first approached him because they had found him listed as a "valuable contact" in the captured wartime records of the so-called Gehlen organization, the Pentagon man said, "We haven't been able to check on that, either. Some of the material in which his name might appear is in our possession, but it's hopelessly mixed up with other captured records, and years of work would be needed to go through it all."

In any case, most sources, inside and outside the Pentagon, agree that, whether or not Wennerström actually was approached by an American agent in Stockholm in 1946, his story of his American Intelligence mission to Leningrad is, at best, a dubious one, and may very well have been part of an attempt to throw dust in the eyes of his interrogators. Such a mission, these sources say, would have been contrary to every security practice of American Intelligence. "If you wanted to get a parcel of, say, radio tubes to an agent in the Soviet Union in 1946, or at any other time, the last thing you would ever do was use a neutral as a courier," a man in "this business" said a while ago. "You would never expose any agent to the dangers involved in such an operation, and you certainly wouldn't use a neutral like Wennerström, because you would have no control over him. In this business, enough thought goes into just the mailing of a single letter to one of your assets [contacts] abroad to make the kind of cowboy approach suggested by Wennerström's account highly improbable. And there are other circumstances to consider. Wennerström says he mailed the parcel in Leningrad to the person to whom it was addressed. There couldn't be a more effective way of exposing an operation. To mail a parcel in any of the major cities in the Soviet Union, including Leningrad, in 1946, you had to take it to a post office and identify yourself to a postal clerk before it would be accepted. The security police would have had agents at the Leningrad post office, and such agents were always on

the lookout for foreigners. In those days, there were
still anti-Soviet partisans in the Baltic woods. In Leningrad then you would probably also have had to open
up any parcel you wanted to mail, and show the postal
people the contents. And even if you did somehow
succeed in mailing your parcel, the chances were that
it would never arrive. People everywhere in the Soviet
Union were extremely poor then, and the pilferage in
the mails was terrible. In short, sending a Wennerström
into the Soviet Union on such a mission at that time
would make sense only if the recipient of the parcel
were someone you wanted to get rid of."

Wennerström's story about his entrance in 1948 into
the Soviet Intelligence apparatus also has its peculiar
aspects, it appears. His account of delivering to Rybachenko, the Soviet air attaché in Stockholm, a map
with just a dot marked on it to indicate the position of
the secret Swedish airfield has a certain plausibility,
and it may be that Wennerström perceived what took
place between him and Rybachenko as he has described it. But the business of deception, whether it
involves the maneuverings of an advertising man preparing a great campaign for some worthless nostrum
or the maneuverings of a man preparing to engage in
espionage against his own country, seems to rest largely
on a foundation of self-deception. It is entirely possible
that Wennerström, in giving military information to
Soviet Intelligence and receiving a fairly good sum of
money—five thousand kronor—in return, succeeded
in persuading himself that his acts did not irrevocably
commit him to the Soviet side—that what he had done
could, in a pinch, be explained to the Swedish authorities, if they found out about it, as a clever attempt
to worm himself into the Soviet Intelligence apparatus
on behalf of his own country and the West.

To the Soviet Intelligence people Wennerström's

activity must have appeared far different from the way it appeared to him. They must have singled him out as a potential recruit some time before the map episode, and it is probable that the talk about a Swedish military airfield was a series of deliberately planned elliptical swings around the subject of Soviet Intelligence needs. It may seem rather remarkable that, out of the whole Swedish officer corps, the Soviet Intelligence operatives should have been able to put the finger on a man who could be prevailed upon to do their work. Yet this insight is not necessarily so exceptional but simply appears to be so because of all the mysterious trappings surrounding the business of intelligence. An example, far removed from that business, of precisely the same sort of acumen is afforded by the people who chose the contestants involved in the television quiz scandals a few years ago. How were they able to pick out almost unerringly, from among many candidates of high intelligence and good education, those who could be counted on to cheat? The answer appears to be that all the contestants chosen had some traits in common. They all had a gnawing desire for public recognition, they all needed money, and they were all willing to move over the barrier of conscience in order to gratify their needs. And these people were chosen not by experts in psychology but by more or less ordinary men in the television-programing business, who could justify their actions on the ground that they were just being practical—just filling a particular demand. The Soviet Intelligence people with whom Wennerström first made contact were not necessarily experts in psychology, either; they were simply experienced at seeking out disaffected citizens, and, in addition, they undoubtedly had at their disposal a good deal of useful information about their man. The Soviet file on Wennerström prob-

ably went back to the early nineteen-thirties, when he
had begun his Russian-language studies in Sweden. In
those days, there were very few Russian-language in-
structors in Sweden, and, according to several Swedes
whose business it is to know such things, Soviet Intelligence almost certainly kept some watch on these
men and their pupils, because of the likelihood that
some members of each group would wind up in intelligence work of one kind or another. Similarly, when
Wennerström obtained a scholarship to study Russian
in Latvia in 1933, and did in fact develop there a
decided interest in intelligence work, Soviet Intelligence was probably aware of it; Riga was a center for
all sorts of intelligence activities concerned with the
Soviet Union, and the Russians kept a sharp watch on
anyone who was likely to have gone there to famil-
iarize himself with Soviet affairs.

Then, in 1940, when Wennerström was assigned to
Moscow as Swedish air attaché, Soviet Intelligence
had a chance to observe him more closely, and through
this surveillance the Russians certainly must have
learned that he had frequent close contact with people
in the German Embassy. They may even have found
out about his intelligence transactions with the Germans—possibly through their own discovery of his
name in captured German documents, since it was with
the help of such documents, plus the interrogation of
captured German Intelligence men, that the Soviets
are believed to have been able to establish, through
blackmail, a considerable part of their postwar espionage network in Western Europe. Furthermore, if
Wennerström's name did indeed turn up in the files
of the Gehlen organization in West Germany after the
war, the Russians probably would also have had access
to that information; the postwar Gehlen organization,
it later turned out, although controlled by the United

States, had been thoroughly penetrated by agents of the Soviet Union and its satellites. Even the director of its counterintelligence activities was found to be a Soviet agent.

When, at last, Wennerström made it plain that he might give Rybachenko information for a price, one of the first questions that Soviet Intelligence must have pondered was whether Wennerström really was trying to do what he later said he had intended to do—insinuate himself into the Soviet Intelligence apparatus in order to undermine it. He was, after all, about to be transferred to Moscow as a Swedish Military Intelligence representative, and, by Soviet reasoning, he might very well have been a *provocateur*. The Russians must have checked on Wennerström's current circumstances very carefully. When they did so, it would not have been difficult for them to discover that he had been refused promotion to a command position in the Swedish Air Force, and thus was likely to be a disappointed man. And the Soviet Intelligence people in Stockholm would know from their own connection with Wennerström that he liked to live well. In Soviet terms, then, Wennerström was a good risk, and whatever plans he might have had for playing a double game with the huge Soviet Intelligence apparatus, the fact was that from the moment he accepted the packet containing the five thousand kronor, he was irrevocably compromised. When the Soviet general whom Nikitushev took him to meet outside Moscow produced the map that Wennerström had passed to Rybachenko in Stockholm, tore it up, and threw it in a wastebasket, with what Wennerström described as "a roguish glint in his eyes," there must have been a world of meaning in that look. It signified to its recipient that Soviet Intelligence was not interested in paying sizable sums merely for dots on maps and that the time had come to get down to business. The Soviet general then asked Wennerström if he wanted to join the Soviet Intelligence service, emphasizing that if he didn't want to join, he could be sure that the subject would never be mentioned again. Whether Wennerström knew it or not, however, he had already been recruited back in Stockholm, and the officer was only going through motions designed to allow Wennerström to accept that fact in a cooperative spirit.

In his account of his surreptitious activities in the Soviet Union, Wennerström maintained that he used his work as an "independent agent" on behalf of the Americans—work that involved his obtaining, in exchange for money and "certain *valuta,*" information on bombing targets within the U.S.S.R.—to further his undercover career with the Soviet Intelligence service. His description of his relationship with the Americans seems on first examination believable enough, but it does not quite tally with the description offered by people in Washington. Wennerström's alleged activities on behalf of the Americans during his Moscow period have been the subject of as thorough an investigation as could be made, and while some of the people concerned concede that he probably did in fact give the Americans some information about Soviet military matters, they say they have been able to satisfy themselves that he never acted as any sort of accredited American agent. A man in the Pentagon said recently, "We've hauled into this headquarters every director of Intelligence, active or retired, who could have had anything to do with Wennerström in Moscow, every attaché who was in Moscow or in Stockholm during or around his Moscow period of service, every key Intelligence officer in Wiesbaden at the time, and officers in other stations as well. We've interrogated all of them exhaustively and checked every payment voucher we could get our hands on, and we've found no evidence that Wennerström ever received any money from our people. Unfortunately, we can't say absolutely that no arrangement with Wennerström *ever* existed, because two of the people who would know are dead. But we have been able to establish to our satisfaction that Wennerström's story of having received payment from us in Italian lire is a fabrication. What he did was to take bits and pieces from somebody else's life story and use them to try to confuse his interrogators by emphasizing that he helped the Americans as well as the Russians.

"Wennerström did give our people some information on a couple of occasions that we know of, but not as a paid agent, or even as an unpaid one. It's perfectly possible, even likely, that if a friendly neutral we know has been traveling in areas of the Soviet Union to which our own people are denied access, we will ask him questions about what he's seen. But that doesn't mean that we sent him on the trip, or had recruited him. To the best of our knowledge, no American organization ever sent Wennerström on any trips, or paid for them, and, as far as we have been able to discover, what he did give us on returning from his trips was quite fragmentary stuff, of no particular value. His drawings of Soviet airplane configurations, for instance, were pretty crude, to tell the truth. Of course, Wennerström's story of handing on information about the pattern of tin roofs in the Ukraine could fit with something we got going around 1949. It was known as Project Wringer, and it consisted of attempting to compile, mostly from interrogations of German prisoners of war returning to Germany from the Soviet Union, very rough simulated radar-target maps of the U.S.S.R. Information on tin roofs is the sort of thing we could have made use of in connection with that project. We have not, however, been able to find any evidence that a target map of the U.S.S.R. like the one described by Wennerström existed in the American Embassy during his Moscow period. It *is* remotely possible that there was some sort of small map that one of our attachés had worked up for himself. And it's conceivable that one of our men could have taken such a map to Air Force headquarters in Wiesbaden for a briefing. We don't think so. But we have no sure check on this, because, again, the two Americans who would really know are dead."

As far as Wennerström's activities on behalf of Soviet Intelligence are concerned, his description of them accords with what a man of his temperament could be expected to perceive or conclude about happenings he was involved with. However, if one looks at his account from the Soviet point of view, the perspective is quite different. The arm of Soviet Intelligence that Wennerström had become involved with was the G.R.U. (Glavnoye Razvedyvatelnoye Upravleniye, or Chief Intelligence Administration)—the military-intelligence service, as distinct from the civilian one, known at present as the K.G.B. (Komiteat Gosudarstvennoi Bezopasnosti, or Committee for State Security). In their world-wide operations, the two organizations carry on a regular competition, and, at times—especially when so ordered from above—an uneasy collaboration. From the moment Wennerström set foot on Soviet soil, he was undoubtedly under continuous close surveillance and study by the G.R.U., and the people he dealt with certainly knew how best to use him.

It was probably no accident that the General, rather than another Soviet officer, was chosen as his principal Soviet Intelligence contact; very likely he was picked as much for his ability to deal with a man of Wennerström's temperament as for his ability to exploit Wennerström's potential for delivering information of importance. It was in keeping with Soviet practice for such a contact to be chosen only after the recruit had been given a trial run by someone else—Nikitushev, in Wennerström's case—who would evaluate his reliability and report on the "feel" of him. The General was what is called in the trade Wennerström's "handler," or "case officer." People in "this business" in Washington are frank in expressing professional admiration of what Wennerström's confession reveals about the General's work. "One notable thing about the Wennerström case is the extraordinary ability of his case officer," a man familiar with the affair has said. Another man has remarked that the General "worked his case beautifully." A handler, or case officer, whatever country he may represent, combines the qualities of an animal trainer and a psychiatrist, and is to the agent he deals with a friend and counselor, a confessor, an impresario, an illusionist, a never-quite-satisfied teacher, and, if he feels the circumstances call for it, a bully and a merciless blackmailer. His sole professional interest is to take a recruited agent and, by any means available, so bend him to his will that the agent is made into the most effective possible instrument of the intelligence service the handler represents.

There is no evidence that the General ever used on Wennerström any of the direct blackmail methods that the Soviet espionage apparatus has often employed—for example, the exploitation of sexual irregularities. His approach seems to have been made with considerable finesse. What he had at his disposal in Wennerström was a man who, for all his outward elegance and social savoir-faire, showed signs—at least to an

able case officer—of being as frustrated in his inner
emotional life as he was in his Air Force career: a man
remote and aloof, unable to maintain, or even make,
intimate contact with other people, preyed upon by
the complex of personal difficulties that passes for
unusual vanity, possessed by an inordinate desire for
recognition, and corroded, under his bland exterior,
by resentment against his Swedish superiors. The depth
of this last feeling was revealed in Wennerström's
bitter aside during the interrogation after his arrest, in
which he said his having been passed over for promotion made him feel "out of the game and made an
exception of. One no longer has any influence, and
hardly anyone pays attention to the views one expresses, et cetera."

When Wennerström met the General, it was as
though he had met someone he had been seeking for
a long time. In the text of Wennerström's pre-trial
examination, the General stands out in vivid fashion,
perhaps less as a personality—a human being with all
sorts of idiosyncrasies—than simply as an extraordinarily strong presence. Upon the stalled personality of
Wennerström, the General must have acted as an en-
ergizing force, one that gave Wennerström the impression of having been granted almost a new opening on
life. From the General, Wennerström received recognition of a worth quite undiscernible to the eyes of
superiors and colleagues. It was certainly not by accident that the G.R.U. assigned to a man whose Air
Force career had been blocked partly because he was
an indifferent flier the grandiose code name Eagle. A
source in Washington has said, "The first thing you
have to do with an agent you have recruited is to build
him up. Build him up, and then chop him down to
size. You need to establish control over him so that
he responds by Pavlovian reflex, almost." The Gen-

eral, when he took over as Wennerström's case officer, sought Wennerström's opinions not just on parochial military matters but on the broad strategic picture. He discussed with him the problem of maintaining the balance of power between East and West, and the chances of preserving world peace through knowledge of the dangers of war. In those days, quite a few neutrals tended to give a sympathetic hearing to the Soviet claim that the U.S.S.R. was being forced into an armaments race by the ring of NATO bases being formed around it, and this kind of argument must have had a powerful effect on Wennerström when he found himself—so he thought—the respected consultant of a Soviet general. People in "this business" in the West tend to find Wennerström's dramatic descriptions of his sessions with the General at "the special headquarters" more a matter for sardonic comment than for uneasiness. One of them has said, "The situation map, the strategic talk, the special headquarters—all this is absolutely standard gamesmanship. It's all part of what you'd expect from an experienced case officer during the process of building up an agent. There are no ground rules, you see. You want your man to feel good, and you can tell him anything he's likely to believe. You want to work him toward a sense of absolute commitment, and, of course, you always want more information out of him." When, during this period in Moscow, the General wanted Wennerström to go out and do some additional spying, he didn't just say he needed more information; he put things in a grander framework. For instance, on the occasion when he told Wennerström that a secret strategic conference of top Soviet military people was soon to be held, and that in order that these authorities might be properly briefed, certain vital data were urgently required, the General observed that Wennerström appeared to be

"the most qualified person" to supply this, adding that
he was relying heavily on Wennerström. Then, when,
according to Wennerström, the General's situation map
"began to show . . . that the essence of NATO's planning
consisted of air strikes against the Soviet Union, but
no invasion," the General didn't just ask Wennerström
to keep on bringing in scraps of information. He told
him that because the Soviet political and military leaders had traditionally thought in terms of a land-based
strategy, "particularly clear proofs" of American intentions would be needed.

It was in response to this request that Wennerström,
by his own account, told the General about the target
map in the United States Embassy and its impending
transfer to Wiesbaden. Of course, it is quite possible
that if such a map existed the G.R.U. managed to
obtain a copy, for Soviet Intelligence has long been
known to employ agents who are particularly skilled
at obtaining such material from couriers or other diplomatic personnel by a variety of means, including
odorless gas capable of rendering victims unconscious.
On occasion, too, Soviet Intelligence operatives have
been known to use drugs on diplomatic personnel. On
March 25, 1964, the United States Marine, Naval, and
Air Attachés in the Soviet Union, along with a British
Assistant Naval Attaché, were simultaneously drugged
at a dinner in Odessa, and when they came to in their
rooms the next day it became apparent that they had
been knocked out soundly enough for a search to have
been made of their effects. However, one circumstance
would tend to argue against the occurrence of something of this sort in connection with the alleged target
map, and that is the General's having told Wennerström how the copy of the map had been obtained—
and telling him only a week after the supposed event.
Soviet security rules dealing with the disclosure to

agents of information about Soviet Intelligence activities are extremely rigid, and infractions of the rules bring ruthless punishment. Thus, if the General came into possession of *any* American target map through Wennerström, he probably did so by means entirely different from those he described.

As for the General's giving Wennerström the authority of a "top agent" and according him the rank of major general in the Soviet Intelligence service, the General probably saw all this in a far different way. For one thing, people familiar with the organization of the G.R.U. declare that there is no such classification as "top agent." "The case officer just invented it to help his man along. The whole thing was just a morale booster," an American in a position to know such things has said. The General's talk about "pair work" probably fell into the same category. Former members of Soviet Intelligence who are now in this country say that such a system simply does not exist. What does exist is the virtuosity of a man like the General when he is working his case. As for Wennerström's being given the rank of major general, a knowledgeable person in Washington has said, "It's quite normal for the Soviets to provide agents with a series of incentive awards that are completely spurious. Perfectly standard operating procedure." After telling Wennerström about his promotion, the General said that from then on, instead of receiving regular payments, he would be entitled to draw sums at will from the treasury of Soviet Intelligence, and could have other sums put in escrow for his future use. That was not a bad bargain from the General's point of view, since Wennerström was expected to draw only reasonable sums for immediate expenses, in order not to arouse the suspicion of his Swedish colleagues. Also Wennerström could reason, as he did during his interrogation, "The less requisitioned for my own use, the more I had to my credit at the final settlement." But as for those sums in escrow, the General must have been well aware that few agents survive to collect such funds.

Despite all the General's talk about strategy, and bases, and the balance of power, and the authority of a "top agent," Wennerström's handler must, during the initial phase, have regarded the colonel as a minor Soviet agent in the Moscow diplomatic community. Soviet Intelligence has a large machine aimed at penetrating foreign embassies in Moscow. Every foreign diplomat, from the moment he is granted a visa to the U.S.S.R., is assigned a case officer by Soviet Intelligence, and from then on, whether he is in the Soviet Union or elsewhere, he is periodically evaluated as a prospective agent. Soviet Intelligence is said to employ ten case officers concerned solely with penetrating the British Embassy. The Intelligence apparatus is able to call on a squad of safecrackers, who boast that they can open almost any safe without leaving traces, and an elaborate network of servant-agents, and it employs complex electronic eavesdropping facilities within embassies and within the diplomats' living quarters. It also employs a squad of experienced *provocateurs* to entrap diplomats and diplomatic employees in compromising situations of one kind or another— usually financial or sexual—and thus recruit them through blackmail. All this is only an extremely small part of the huge internal and external Soviet Intelligence and security apparatus, civilian and military, which, it is estimated, employs at least a quarter of a million people. In relation to this vast organization, Wennerström's espionage activities while he was in the Soviet Union were probably modest indeed. He had no access to really secret information at the American Embassy, for the attachés he knew there weren't policy-makers but people who relayed back to the United States such scraps of information about the Soviet Union as their highly restricted movements allowed them to pick up. It seems probable that Wennerström was chosen for a rather extensive buildup not so much because of the comparatively small amount of information he might be able to glean from Allied diplomats in Moscow as because the G.R.U. recognized that, as Swedish air attaché, he was likely sooner or later to be transferred to duty in some Allied capital, and might well wind up in some senior diplomatic post in Stockholm. In other words, the G.R.U. was interested in him primarily as a long-term investment. As an agent "in place" he was in the network for life— or until he was caught.

In the U.S.S.R., Wennerström's activities were certainly under very careful scrutiny and control. He may have believed that he traveled unobserved to Leningrad to photograph the material on metal alloys, but the probability is, according to people familiar with the Soviet security system, that the trail he followed was efficiently blazed for him by Soviet Intelligence, which had every interest in giving him a helping hand up the Swedish diplomatic ladder. The length to which Soviet Intelligence will go to make a recruited agent more useful to his own government often is remarkable. And, indeed, his apparent efficiency on the job in Moscow had much to do with his superiors' eventual decision to transfer him to Washington. Whether he traveled to the Ukraine or along the Murmansk railway, he was under surveillance not only as a foreign military attaché—and nobody in the Soviet Union is kept under tighter surveillance than a foreign military attaché, neutral or not—but also as a Soviet agent who might be a double agent for the West. He must have been followed relentlessly. Under the influence of the General, Wennerström seems to have behaved like a man in a trance. Someone familiar with the Wennerströms of this world has remarked, "Agents are very neurotic individuals who are likely to turn on you at any time. And they're likely to get out of hand very easily during the building-up process. In this business, there's a saying that either the case officer controls the agent or the agent controls the case officer. The Russians sum it up in an old Bolshevik phrase, 'Kto, kogo,'—meaning 'Who [over] whom.' You have to control your man very carefully every step of the way. You have to show him unmistakably who's master."

Whatever double game Wennerström may have attempted to play during his period in Moscow, the G.R.U. people must have had a pretty good idea of it, and they certainly made use of this information at a time of their own choosing. It can hardly have been mere coincidence that the dramatic confrontation between the General and Wennerström occurred shortly before Wennerström's transfer to Washington. The General, necessarily recognizing that when the transfer took place, the G.R.U. would no longer be able to exert complete physical control over Wennerström's activities, chose a time just before his departure to impress upon him unforgettably the realization that Soviet Intelligence was no organization to be trifled with. When Wennerström was given the terrifying news that the Russians had broken the American code and had found his name mentioned as an informant on Soviet military matters, what was being put on for Wennerström was a play in which he was made the central character. The General's story about breaking the American code was almost certainly made up out of whole cloth. If such a code-breaking feat really had been achieved, the fact would have been concealed by the tightest security precautions possible, and if a Soviet Intelligence officer had ever gone as far as to reveal such a secret to a man accused of being a double agent, the officer would unquestionably have been shot. (So, in Stalinist times, would anybody associated with him in committing such an error; and his family would probably have been sent to Siberia.) Soviet Intelligence people have been known to be sentenced to terms in Siberia for such lapses as forgetting to lock a safe.

An American familiar with such matters said recently, "The story of the code's being broken is just the kind of thing you could expect from Wennerström's case officer. It's the kind of thing that happens constantly in this business. When you need to impress an agent with your omniscience, you go to elaborate lengths to do so. Of course, Wennerström had no way of knowing that the Russians *hadn't* broken the American code, or that his name *hadn't* been used in a radio message, but we've been unable to find the slightest evidence that his name ever was so used. Wennerström accepted on faith what his handler told him. Whatever real evidence the Russians might have had on hand about any tips given by Wennerström to the Americans in Moscow had probably been acquired through the usual G.R.U. surveillance—conceivably through their routine bugging of the American offices and residential quarters in Moscow. The G.R.U. people wouldn't necessarily use this kind of compromising material right away. One striking thing about the Soviet Intelligence system is its infinite patience. Wennerström's case officer doubtless waited for just the right moment to use the material on Wennerström. To build the agent up and cut him down so that he responds just as you want him to respond requires, among other things, a keen sense of timing."

The results of that dramatic confrontation were admirably successful, from the General's point of view. Wennerström later indicated that he was immensely grateful to the General at the time for being "heart and soul on my side." Thus, Wennerström was able to emerge from the confrontation feeling immense relief, extreme respect for the long arm of Soviet Intelligence, and increased devotion toward the General.

Notwithstanding the General's impressive talk about the great contribution that Wennerström could make in the realm of global strategy, the tasks that the G.R.U. set for him in Washington were severely limited. Thus, the General told him that Soviet Intelligence was not interested in material on the composition of American military forces. Nor was Wennerström to concern himself with nuclear weapons; in this respect, he later quoted the General as saying, the Russians "had confidence for the most part in their own strength." What the General really wanted from Wennerström was technical information on the development of aircraft and related equipment; he knew very well that, as a neutral attaché, Wennerström had little access to classified information in the Pentagon or anywhere else. He was probably content to use Wennerström mainly for passing on technical material to which Soviet and Soviet-satellite military attachés didn't have ready access. The fact that much of the material wasn't classified didn't mean that it wasn't useful; some of it may have been very valuable to Soviet technicians. Wennerström had a very good cover as a diplomat, and had every reason for visiting aircraft plants, and so on, in areas where Soviet diplomats weren't allowed, and the General apparently saw to it that he didn't get out of hand and make a blunder of the sort that would end his espionage career.

Wennerström's native caution helped. "As we look at Wennerström's pattern of activity in this country, it's apparent to us that he must have collected only about a hundredth of what he *could* have collected when he was here," a Pentagon official who knows a great deal about the Wennerström affair said recently. "He certainly wasn't aggressive about asking for information. He requested from us only a few things that were classified, and, to our knowledge, he received nothing classified from the Pentagon until quite late in his service here. Most of what he got for the Swedes consisted of Air Force manuals and large numbers of industrial brochures and technical papers, and just about everything that he got for the Swedes he passed on to the Russians, too. Wennerström wasn't very discriminating about what he passed along. We now have a pretty good idea what it consisted of, and you have to have read through this material to realize how trifling much of it was. But the Russians obviously weren't unhappy to have it coming in, and I can see their point. I'd like to have a source like that myself in a couple of places I can think of.

"To judge from the visits that Wennerström made to industrial plants and Air Force bases here, the Russians were cautious about pushing him too hard. Wennerström was not the least bit conspicuous about his travels, and he gave us no reason to be suspicious of him. As a friendly neutral diplomat, he wasn't subjected to surveillance. You have to be very selective about surveillance in any case, because of the shortage of manpower, and because, after all, this isn't a police state. In the Soviet Union, the security apparatus has complete control over all the trains, all the planes, all the hotels—everything. We have nothing like that here. The average person doesn't realize the complexity of maintaining proper surveillance of a military attaché,

who is apt to be always on the move. It takes a min-
imum of nine men on a direct tail, outside of the
additional backup men needed, and if your man is
traveling across the country, you have to cover his
airplane stops en route to make sure he doesn't get
off, and when he does, you have to anticipate all sorts
of tricks, such as his leaving word with room service
to call him at six and then slipping away at four by
way of the freight elevator. Also, you have to rely in
part on cooperation from local law-enforcement agencies, and such cooperation can vary from outstanding
to nil. There are a couple of hundred attachés and
assistant attachés in Washington, and we have our
work cut out just keeping track of Soviet diplomatic
personnel, of whom as many as eighty per cent are
case officers or handlers of one sort or another. Also,
in the Iron Curtain embassies there are all the chauf-
feurs, cleaning people, and so on, some of whom have
been known to stand higher on the Party lists than
some of the diplomats. We had no evidence that gave
us reason to put a tail on Wennerström. Soviet Intelligence just kept him going quietly, in a generally small
way. They never had him step out of character, and
eventually, when, in his official capacity as chief of
the Swedish Air Force Purchasing Mission here, he
was able to get his hands on highly classified information about the Bomarc and HM-55 missiles, the
Russians had a tremendous windfall. Apart from this,
as far as we have been able to determine, Wennerström
gave them only routine technical stuff while he was
here."

People in the Pentagon have conceded that it is
reasonable to assume that, just as Wennerström has
claimed, when he arrived in this country he was in-
terviewed by Intelligence officers concerning his experiences in the Soviet Union, but they maintain that

such an interview would have consisted only of the routine kind of debriefing that is accorded friendly travelers coming from the U.S.S.R. As for the story Wennerström told his interrogators of having twice acted as a paid courier for the C.I.A. in Washington, this, say our Intelligence people, in inherently implausible, and was probably intended to confuse his Swedish interrogators. Of course, anything can happen in the world of espionage, and a man in the Pentagon has said, "It *is* conceivable that the Agency felt they were dealing with something sensitive enough not to let us know about it when we were making our investigation." But Wennerström's story of acting for the C.I.A. does seem highly unlikely, for three reasons. The first is that, in keeping with the same security consideration that made Wennerström's story of having engaged in intelligence activities for the Americans in 1946 look so dubious, the C.I.A. would almost certainly never endanger the life of any agent it might have in the Soviet Embassy in Washington by making casual use of a neutral like Wennerström as a middleman. The second reason, which involves the sum that Wennerström said he received for passing on the packages, seems even more persuasive. According to the Pentagon man, "Payment of a sum like a thousand dollars is simply fantastic for the kind of job Wennerström described. You would *never* pay out that sort of money unless you intended to compromise the guy. And to pay a sum like that twice over would be doubly ridiculous." The third reason for doubting Wennerström was advanced by a colleague of the man in the Pentagon: "In his interrogation, Wennerström said that he couldn't recall all the passwords used by his opposite number in the encounter with the supposed contact in the Soviet Embassy. To me, this means that his story of the meeting is a fabrication. I never met

a man in this business who couldn't remember a recognition signal years after the meeting in which it had
been used. These signals are far too important to the
lives of agents to slip out of the mind like that."

The process of controlling Wennerström in Washington was made easier for the G.R.U. by the home
leaves he had in 1953 and 1955, during which he
attended secret meetings in Helsinki when the General
was able to give him new instructions directly and to
size up his state of mind. The fact that during one of
these meetings Wennerström was asked to fill out the
paper that the General said was an application for
Soviet citizenship—in order that the Russians could
bail him out if he should be caught as a spy, he was
told—is regarded by people familiar with the case as
indicative primarily of the General's estimate of Wennerström's feelings at the time. "The business of Soviet
citizenship probably was intended as just another morale booster for Wennerström, who may have expressed some anxiety to his handler about the activities
of our Counterintelligence people in Washington," one
man has said, adding, "The Russians never *would* get
him out of trouble, of course, but it cost the handler
nothing to have Wennerström fill out the form. And
since the application requires a photograph of the ap-
plicant, the handler must have been at least able to
supply himself with an up-to-date picture of his agent
for the G.R.U. files."

Whatever Wennerström's usefulness as an agent
during his time in the United States, there seems to
be little doubt that his broadest acts of espionage against
any one country occurred later, in Sweden. The General, in spite of his constant assurances that Soviet
Intelligence had no particular interest in Swedish affairs, had probably suspected from the very beginning

that Wennerström's ultimate value would lie in just this area. Even though Wennerström had been imbued with bitterness against the Americans just before he left Moscow, he does not seem to have gone about his espionage in the United States with any great personal animus against this country. A man in Washington has observed, "An experienced case officer knows that an agent is always at his most effective when he is working against his own country. You get an agent under strongest control in regard to something he feels ambivalent about." So, in meeting after meeting over the years, the General had told Wennerström that the only thing about Sweden that interested him was whether it was adhering to its policy of neutrality in the Cold War. And when Wennerström was transferred from Washington to Stockholm, the General harped on the theme even more insistently. And it was Sweden that Wennerström, step by step, betrayed most sweepingly. It was as though he were able to keep his acts against his own country in a certain section of his mind, like airplanes circling in a perpetual hold at a given altitude on orders from a control tower. As he continued to commit his acts of espionage, giving away secret after secret until he had compromised the entire Swedish air-defense system, he seems to have allowed himself to believe that he was really acting as a world strategist, and one who possessed power—recognized by only one other man—almost great enough to change the angle of the earth's axis. Wherever Wennerström went, and whatever he did, the General was his secret sharer. The reports about his daily life which Wennerström wrote to the General from Washington and Stockholm by his own account transcended mere business communications, and became more deeply personal in tone as time went on. It was the General who proposed that Wennerström write such letters, and he must have been well aware that they were of psychological as well as material importance in his handling of Wennerström. A man familiar with "this business" has said, "The encouraging of such letters is part of the case officer's design for bringing his agent into complete personal subjection. There are practical considerations involved: the agent may not be smart enough to know what's really going on, and might miss all sorts of opportunities that the case officer would spot, and the letters are very useful to the case officer in this respect. And in having the agent acquire the habit of writing these letters, you, as the handler, are taking another step toward establishing complete mastery over him. You're God, and the agent must understand that he can fulfill himself only by doing just what you tell him to. The most important things in the life of an agent are the meetings with his case officer. You'd have to have been involved in such meetings to realize fully the extraordinary yearning passion with which the agent looks forward to them. The handler, being the man who understands the agent's life and his problems best, is sometimes greeted with an emotion so intense as to be comparable, I should say, only to young love. When Wennerström was unable to meet his case officer at frequent intervals, he was in the position of an addict in need of a fix. Writing the letters to the General became a substitute for the meetings. He *had* to write to his case officer, in order to keep himself going."

What Wennerström received in return for these letters, which gave the General what Wennerström later called a "complete insight into my whole life," consisted merely of further espionage instructions, brief thanks for secrets received, and, occasionally, birthday or New Year's greetings "and such banal things." Another man familiar with the Wennerström affair has observed—without meaning to express professional disrespect toward the General—that the emotional attachment an agent feels for his case officer is altogether out of proportion to the stature of the person the agent is working for. Wennerström found the General entirely fascinating, and yet the General emerges from Wennerström's account more as a force than as an individual. It is unlikely that the General was a sparkling conversationalist, for example, since the spontaneity that gives rise to such a talent can be dangerous to a career officer in the Soviet Intelligence apparatus. The skilled manipulation of Wennerström was undoubtedly made possible largely by the exalted qualities with which Wennerström endowed the General and everything connected with him. Wennerström's account of his fifteen years of espionage for the Soviet Union is somehow too neat, too clean-cut, too much like a description of a chess game, to ring completely true. It lacks that peculiar grubby quality that shows through all sorts of other accounts of Soviet espionage, such as the accounts in the Royal Commission report on the Soviet atomic-spy ring uncovered in Canada in 1946, and the accounts given in the late David J. Dallin's *Soviet Espionage,* a standard scholarly work on the subject. What made that soiled world seem clean in Wennerström's account was not only the General's persuasive force but his skill in exploiting Wennerström's readiness to imagine things as he would like them to be.

Wennerström prided himself on being regarded as a Soviet expert, and yet he hardly ever opened a serious book on any subject except purely technical aviation matters. What he did read, mainly, was spy stories. To most people who read such stories the fantasies they engage in while they are reading are recognizable as such, and the fantasies fade away when the book is finished and they turn once again to the real world.

But with Wennerström, such fantasies apparently did not possess this evanescent quality. It was the capacity to act out his daydreams, and act them out endlessly, that made Wennerström such a useful spy. He somehow managed to go on believing in the exalted nature of his role—to go on thinking of himself as the "top agent" secretly called upon in great international crises to help turn the world toward peace. He said later that the General constantly impressed upon him that "the risk of war really consisted in the making of a wrong appraisal in crisis situations." And he was particularly gratified by the notion that his appraisals increased his prestige with his Soviet superiors, as when he was told, for instance, that some information he had delivered on the Berlin crisis "had given rise to a special memorandum of appreciation."

A more realistic picture of Wennerström's role and of how his contributions in times of crisis were regarded by Soviet Intelligence can be gained from his account of the help he gave the Russians during the Lebanon crisis, when he reported the abrupt departure of the American general from Wiesbaden. The General never seems to have dreamed for a moment of telling his close collaborator—the major general in Soviet Intelligence, the man armed with "the top Soviet agent's authority"—what was really afoot at that time. It was "only through subsequent incidents" that Wennerström learned that the American general's departure was connected with the Lebanon crisis. When Wennerström was let in on a "secret," it was always safely after the event, if indeed the event ever occurred. When the meeting he was to have had with the General in Vienna in June 1962 was postponed, only later did he find out the "reason." The General, he was told, had been in Cuba, directing Soviet Intelligence activities in the period preceding the Cuban missile crisis. But the fact is that if the General had been in Cuba directing Soviet Intelligence activities, Wennerström would have been the last man in the world to know about it. It would have been folly for a Soviet Intelligence officer to commit such a breach of security with such an agent. The story of the General's activities in Cuba was simply an artistic touch designed to let Wennerström believe that it took the Cuban crisis to keep him and the General apart.

When the Cuban crisis arrived, and Wennerström provided the G.R.U. with a report that he believed was pertinent to American intentions in Cuba, he later said, with some pride, that about a month afterward he received a message telling him that "the chief of the [Soviet Military] Intelligence service, whom I had met in 1960 in Moscow, conveyed his special thanks for the information." What did this mean? A set of events like the Cuban crisis brings forth all sorts of people who allow themselves to believe that they have played a crucial role in connection with it. Wennerström may well have believed that his actions contributed to saving the peace during the crisis. The late Dr. Stephen Ward, the osteopath in the famous Profumo affair, was no Soviet agent, but he liked to think that, by repeating among his Mayfair and Whitehall acquaintances various bits of talk he had picked up from a Russian diplomat during the Cuban missile crisis, he was helping to save the peace, too.

"During the Cuban crisis, the Soviet apparatus, as you might expect, flooded the network with demands for information and the net poured it back," a man who knows "this business" said a while ago. "Later on, when the handlers had the time, they told the agents, 'That was great, very useful.' Of course, most of it was garbage." Wennerström seems to have been particularly gratified at having received thanks for his work in the Cuban crisis directly from "the chief of the Soviet Military Intelligence service"—presumably the same four-star general from whom he received the medals rewarding him for his long and fruitful service. Wennerström was very proud of meeting that four-star general, whose name, if he knew it, he did not give his Swedish interrogators. In 1960, as it happens, there was only one four-star general in the G.R.U., and that was General Ivan Aleksandrovich Serov, its supreme commander. Considering the probability that every award Wennerström had previously received from the G.R.U.—the rank of major general, the "authority of a top agent"—was spurious, there is no reason to believe that the decorations he was told he was being given weren't spurious, too. Nor is there any reason to believe that the man who decorated him was Serov. Since there would hardly be much point in having a real four-star general take the time to present fake decorations to a fake major general, the strong probability is that the four-star general was also a fake. The real decorations are reserved for thoroughgoing professionals, like the Soviet Intelligence officer Colonel Rudolf Abel, who served for many years in this country as an "illegal"; who, after being caught, confessed to nothing at all; and who was eventually exchanged for Francis Gary Powers, the American U-2 pilot captured in the U.S.S.R. Only recently Abel was made a Hero of the Soviet Union. In other words, the ceremony decorating Wennerström for his services to the Soviet Union was probably just another little playlet put on by the General for the sake of Wennerström's morale.

The remarkable thing about the handling of Wennerström is the extraordinary effect that sheer secrecy—secret actions, a sense of secret power, and secret recognition—had upon him. It was as though, for him, secrecy became almost an end in itself, so that, as far as his acts against his own country were concerned, he derived what he referred to as a "deep inner satisfaction" not merely from their commission but also from the realization that the people around him did not know he was committing them. Wennerström seems to have become possessed by secrecy. In more than one sense, it was the means he used to try to keep himself alive. Of course, Wennerström's long career as a spy was made possible by the almost perfect legal cover under which he operated and his undoubted technical skill at camouflage. But of all the camouflages he used, the most effective involved not the employment of his diplomatic position to conceal his espionage but rather his espionage itself. For it is his espionage that Wennerström seems to have used as a cover story in his complex transactions with his inner self. And it fell to the General to reinforce this cover story and to help make it stick by imparting to Wennerström's self-estrangement the illusion of large purpose and design.

It is a tribute to the talents of the General and an indication of the power of Wennerström's capacity for self-deception that after his arrest and interrogation he could not bring himself to assert that he had been anything less than a "top agent." Whereas another man charged with participation in a criminal conspiracy might well have claimed that he was a mere bystander, or, at most, a small cog in the machine, Wennerström could not lower himself to any such level. Nor, apparently, could he allow himself to manifest any doubts about the integrity of the people who had so long manipulated him. "The Soviet Intelligence service functions like precision clockwork. There is no question of its cheating any of its members," he said stiffly when asked during his pre-trial examination whether he was quite sure that the Russians would, in fact, have settled hundreds of thousands of kronor on him if he had so requested the General. Not only did Wennerström admit that he was indeed a spy but he established himself as the most important spy in all Swedish history. He damned himself with a thoroughness that no single witness, no series of witnesses, no prosecutor could match, and so went down fascinated to the last with the idea of secret power.

Seven

W HEN A SPY HAS BEEN CAUGHT, ONE OF THE IMME-
diate consequences is that the intelligence services of
both the country he has spied for and the country or
countries he has spied against set up what are known
as Damage Assessment Committees to determine the
degree to which their own military and espionage systems have been compromised. Of the various periods
of Wennerström's career as a spy, the one that the
Pentagon people believe to have been least harmful to
the United States was his term of service as Swedish
air attaché in Moscow in the late nineteen-forties and
the early fifties. During his years in the United States,
he gave the Russians a great deal of routine information
and pulled off two important coups—supplying Soviet
Intelligence with the plans and specifications for the
Bomarc and HM-55 missiles. Though these weapons
systems may now be relatively unimportant, the technical insights he afforded the Russians cannot be taken

back. These insights relate not only to the mechanisms
he actually reported on but also to those of later missile
systems, because a thorough examination by experts
of the way in which design problems are approached
in one such weapon enables the experts to predict the
characteristics of later ones.

As for Wennerström's final espionage period, in
Sweden, the Swedes believe that he gravely compromised their defense system, and it is probable that as
a result an entirely new system of interlocking radar
and anti-aircraft missile sites has had to be organized.
Thanks to a great deal of painstaking work—for example, the examination of thousands of documents to
determine whether they had been restapled, as an indication of whether he unstapled them in order to photograph them page by page—the Swedes have, they
feel, a very good idea of what he could have given
the Russians, and their general estimate is that, in view
of the rapid rate of obsolescence of modern electronic
equipment, the damage to their defense system, while
very serious, is something short of catastrophic.

Certainly the damage done by Wennerström to Sweden's defense capability is less, in the view of people
in Washington, than the damage done to the Soviet
defense system by Colonel Oleg Penkovsky, a Soviet
Military Intelligence officer who was shot by the Russians in 1963 as a Western agent. Penkovsky appears
to have been a kind of Wennerström for the West in
the Soviet Union. Although the complete authenticity
of a book bearing Penkovsky's name has been chal-
lenged by Sovietologists, Penkovsky was undoubtedly
an agent of first importance. He held a fairly responsible position in the G.R.U. and was a senior official
of a Soviet committee coordinating intelligence on scientific research, including rocket research. Penkovsky,
who, like Wennerström, passed great quantities of se-

cret intelligence to his foreign principals on microfilm, is said to have severely compromised the entire Soviet inter-continental-ballistic-missile system, and to have cost the Soviets the equivalent of billions of dollars in the process.

Like Wennerström, Penkovsky volunteered his services to the other side in the Cold War, and it seems that, as was the case of Wennerström, his acts of espionage took place against the background of a blocked career and a smoldering resentment against his superiors. It is quite probable that Penkovsky, as a disappointed man, was manipulated by his Western case officers almost as thoroughly as Wennerström was by the General. However, the motivations of the two spies are not comparable in respect to ideology. Wennerström's espionage certainly does not seem to have had any ideological foundation. Nor does he seem to have been given any noticeable degree of indoctrination by his case officer during his long years of service for the Soviet Union. The General was not interested in introducing Wennerström to Marxist dialectics; this, from the General's point of view, would only have increased the risk of Wennerström's letting slip phrases having a pro-Soviet tinge. The General was interested only in getting as much information as he could out of Wennerström. So little does the latter seem to have involved himself with ideological considerations that in the thousands of pages of interrogation concerning his espionage work there is, for instance, no indication of Joseph Stalin's ever having lived or died. As for Communism itself, Wennerström told his interrogators that while it might be suitable for certain other countries, he didn't think it would be a good thing for Sweden. His acts against his country, he insisted, were solely in the service of peace. Penkovsky believed that, too, but, as Westerners are bound to see it, with better

reason. Whereas Wennerström committed his most serious espionage against one of the most truly democratic countries on earth—his own—Penkovsky's
espionage was committed against the background of a
conspiratorial society, and was directed against the
leadership of a huge authoritarian state. The damage
to the military position of the Soviets caused by Penkovsky's activities had much greater immediate effects
on the state of the world than did Wennerström's espionage. When, in mid-October 1962, as the Cuban
missile crisis was drawing to a climax, U-2 planes
were able successfully to make photographic reconnaissance of western Cuba, it was information from
microfilms already passed along by Penkovsky that
enabled United States experts to ascertain just what
type of missiles the Soviets were putting into place
and how great a potential threat they would be. The
amount of microfilming that Penkovsky had devoted
to these weapons alone was at least as great as Wennerström had put in on the Bomarc and HM-55 missiles. The manuals on the Bomarc that Wennerström
photographed in Washington and later in Sweden
amounted to a pile of documents perhaps a foot and
a half high. But the microfilms that Penkovsky delivered to the West concerning the entire Soviet missile
arsenal may have represented enough secret documents
to fill up a wallful of safes. Penkovsky's capture ("Like
Wennerström, he bugged out too late," a man in the
Pentagon has remarked) led to a wholesale shakeup in
the hierarchy of the Soviet Intelligence service. And
one of the victims of the shakeup was General Serov,
who was thrown out of office in 1963 and was igno-
miniously expelled from the Party two years later.

Who the members of the Soviet Damage Assessment Committee on the Wennerström case were could

probably be guessed at from a review of the comings and goings of Soviet diplomatic personnel in Stockholm shortly after Wennerström's arrest. (Of course, he compromised the Russians to the extent of informing on his local Soviet contacts in Stockholm, and, consequently, First Secretary Georgi Baranovsky and Military Attaché Vitaly Nikolsky were each declared *persona non grata* by the Swedes and had to leave the country.) During their studies, the members of the Soviet Damage Assessment Committee must have considered the possibility that the Swedish security people, when they began to close in on Wennerström, had taken the precaution of putting some false secret documents in his way. To resolve this question, the G.R.U. would have had to check on the authenticity of the documents it had lately received from Wennerström—research that would most likely have entailed a further round of spying on the Swedes.

While it prepared the ground for such further rounds of spying, the Soviet Damage Assessment Committee was not itself immune from scrutiny. The composition of such a committee is a matter of considerable interest to its counterparts on the opposite side, because the choice of those conducting the investigation sometimes affords indications of particular areas in which the investigation is likely to be pressed, or of what use is likely to be made of the findings. For instance, the committee members would very likely have attempted to sort out information regarding matters that they believed might compromise other Soviet espionage operations—for example, information about the secret process used for developing the microfilm used by Wennerström, which may or may not have been successfully analyzed by the Swedish security people. This information would be put into two files by the committee. One file would be used as a basis for reinforcing the security of the espionage system; agents would be given a different kind of film, for instance. The other file would be for the use of *provocateurs* trying to penetrate Western Intelligence organizations. These agents could offer the developing formula of the sort of film used by Wennerström to representatives of the West for the purpose of establishing, at the least cost to the Soviets, the *provocateurs'* bona fides as informants. In view of such possibilities, it must have been particularly interesting to Western intelligence experts when they established that the Soviet Damage Assessments Committee on the Wennerström affair was headed by a K.G.B. officer who traveled under the name of Ivan Ivanovich Avalov. In reality, Avalov is Ivan Ivanovich Agayants, an experienced Intelligence officer who is head of Department D of the First Main Directorate, the foreign-operations arm of the K.G.B.—the post-mortem on the Wennerström case being automatically under the jurisdiction of the K.G.B., which maintains over-all control of matters involving compromises of security information. In the table of organization of the First Main Directorate (a lineup that includes a grimly numbered Section 13, which handles assassinations and other matters that Soviet Intelligence men refer to by the slang expression "wet affairs"), Department D stands for *"dezinformatsiia"*—literally, "disinformation." Department D is devoted to specialized activities known in Washington under the heading of "deception and confusion." In fact, Department D is a central clearing house for lies and diversionary material manufactured and processed by the various arms of Soviet Intelligence. It is a coordinating body that sees to it that, for example, a spurious document turned out in Moscow and passed along to Soviet agents in South America as part of an elaborate scheme for misleading or penetrating Western intelligence services there is confirmed by another document produced by other Soviet agents in Japan and is reinforced by a third set of alleged facts introduced into the appropriate channels by another source in Europe. The discovery of Agayants' involvement must have alerted Western intelligence people for Department D operations in the aftermath of the Wennerström affair.

It appears that Baranovsky and Nikolsky were not the only Soviet officers compromised—or "burned," as the trade expression goes—by the Wennerström affair. People in "this business" in Washington have interested themselves in Wennerström's good friend the General. And—with no help from Wennerström— they have finally succeeded in finding out just who he is. One of the pertinent facts they have uncovered about the General appears to be that during Wennerström's years in Moscow and the United States, and, in fact, up to the time Wennerström's retirement from the Swedish Air Force in 1957, the General was not a general at all but a colonel, like Wennerström himself. He is known as a very able G.R.U. officer with a fair command of English, who has operated under many names besides Lemenov. As Pavel Petrovich Mikhailov, from 1941 to 1945, he was Soviet Vice-Consul in New York, and in 1945 he was made Acting Consul. In 1942 and 1943, under the code name Molière, he helped establish the Soviet atomic-espionage network in Canada that was exposed in 1946 by the defecting Soviet code clerk Igor Gouzenko. At the end of 1943, having completed his Canadian assignment, Mikhailov took over a Soviet espionage network in the United States known as the S. & T. network, which had formerly been run by a man known as Arthur A. Adams, a G.R.U. "illegal" who was never caught. Mikhailov is also known to have been involved in the

transfer of Soviet secret funds from this side of the
Atlantic to an important Second World War spy network in Switzerland run, at the time of Mikhailov's
involvement with it, by a woman agent named Rahel
Dubendorfer. He left this country in 1946 as a result
of the Gouzenko revelations. Before he left, he made
approaches to Albert Einstein to try to persuade him
to take up residence in East Germany. In addition to
operating under the name of Mikhailov, Wennerström's General was also known as Fyodor Petrovich
Malin, a name under which he did a good deal of
traveling in Western Europe, in the capacity of a Coun-
sellor at the Soviet Ministry of Foreign Affairs, between 1957 and 1962. His real name, however, is
Pyotr Pavlovich Melkishev. He is sixty-four. Photographs of him taken at various times show him to be
stocky, gray-haired, and full-lipped, with a wide mouth
drawn downward in a determined way, a strong square
jaw, and very cool eyes.

Although Wennerström was led to believe that the
General belonged to the American sector of the Soviet
Military Intelligence organization during his period of
contact with him, actually this was not the case at all.
Melkishev belonged, until 1958, to the Second Directorate, which is the European sector. (Espionage against
the United States is handled by the Third Directorate.)
In the first part of 1958, he was made Deputy Chief
of the Second Directorate; and late in 1958, having at
last really become a general officer, he was made chief
of the Fourth Directorate of the G.R.U., which is
concerned with Near and Far Eastern territory extend-
ing from Egypt to Burma. He was undoubtedly busying
himself with that area when Wennerström believed him
to be in Cuba. Wennerström testified that his old friend
said that he was being kept on in the Intelligence service to work with Wennerström until they could retire

together. But now, with Wennerström no longer active as a Soviet agent, the General is still hard at it. When he was promoted from colonel to general, he continued as Wennerström's principal case officer, probably in part because of the established effectiveness of their relationship and in part just to keep his hand in. He would keep himself briefed on Wennerström's activities, but he almost certainly arranged for most of the communications received from Wennerström during this time to be processed by a colleague, whose acknowledgments and further instructions were then relayed to Wennerström.

As for Wennerström, his situation is quite gloomy. He is lodged in solitary confinement, under maximum-security conditions, in Långholmen Prison, in Stockholm, where he is No. 991. The methodical Swedes, having discovered the absence of the horse, have now made an elaborate show of locking the barn door. Wennerström, their most important state prisoner, lives in a soundproof cell that is said to have been specially reconstructed for him, with walls a foot and a half thick. He is not allowed to talk to any other prisoners, on the theory that he might divulge some vital defense secret. He is kept under constant surveillance and subjected to frequent searches by a special group of guards, who are forbidden to converse with him. He seems to have aged greatly in prison. Some time ago, an article in the Stockholm newspaper *Expressen* reported that he had been assigned a prison job folding and gluing paper to make envelopes. The article also reported that his morale was very low, and that he complained bitterly because the prison authorities wouldn't assign him a clerical job and give him a typewriter, as they had promised. He was especially pained by this, it appeared, because he needed a typewriter in order to work on his memoirs—the memoirs of a top Soviet agent. He has since got his typewriter, and he has written at least part of the memoirs, in the form of letters to his wife. Besides his prison work and letter writing, he has been doing a certain amount of reading. Part of it consists of technical aviation magazines, but what he still reads mostly, it seems, is spy thrillers.

11   TA-4

More undercover activity from...

The Ballantine Espionage/Intelligence Library

True stories of international espionage that read like the best espionage thrillers...

FOR YOUR EYES ONLY!

TA-9